SAMS
Teach Yourself

PC Upgrades

by Galen A. Grimes

in 10 Minutes

SAMS

A Division of Macmillan Computer Publishing
201 West 103rd St., Indianapolis, Indiana 46290 USA

©1998 by Sams Publishing

International Standard Book Number: 0-672-31323-5

Library of Congress Catalog Card Number: 98-84600

00 99 98   8 7 6 5 4 3 2 1

Interpretation of the printing code: the rightmost number of the first series of numbers is the year of the book's printing; the rightmost number of the second series of numbers is the number of the book's printing. For example, a printing code of 98-1 shows that the first printing of the book occurred in 1998.

Screen reproductions in this book were created by means of the program Collage Plus from Inner Media, Inc., Hollis, NH.

Printed in the United States of America

Publisher John Pierce

Executive Editor Jim Minatel

Managing Editor Thomas F. Hayes

Acquisitions Editor Jill Byus

Development Editor Rick Kughen

Technical Editor Russ Jacobs

Production Editor Lori A. Lyons

Copy Editor Tom Stevens

Editorial Assistant Jennifer L. Chisholm

Book Designer Kim Scott

Cover Designer Dan Armstrong

Indexer Tim Tate

Production Team Angela Calvert, Kim Cofer

CONTENTS

INTRODUCTION

You've made a major investment in your PC and you want to continue using it for as long as possible. But nearly every week it seems you are bombarded with news about the newest whiz-bang, mega-sized, super-duper, hyper-accelerated 8,000 MegaHertz model PC just rolling off the assembly line. All of a sudden, the box on your desk in front of you doesn't seem quite as powerful, and you are wondering if it's time to take out a loan for a new PC.

WELCOME TO *SAMS' TEACH YOURSELF PC UPGRADES IN 10 MINUTES*

Instead of buying a new PC, you may be able to extend the useful lifespan of your existing PC simply by upgrading a few of the existing components.

This book (like all the books in the *Sams' Teach Yourself in 10 Minutes* series) is a streamlined introduction to upgrading your PC. It will give you everything you need to know in order to replace your CPU, motherboard, hard disk drives, memory, and just about any component in your PC—and it's done in small, easy-to-use lessons.

Each lesson is designed to give you the skills and tools you need to get through your personal, online agenda in 10 minutes or less. You can learn on a need-to-know basis, skipping from lesson to lesson, or you may want to sit down and plow through the whole thing from cover to cover. What you learn, and when you learn it, is left up to you and your needs.

HOW TO USE *SAMS' TEACH YOURSELF PC UPGRADES IN 10 MINUTES*

If you're starting from scratch, start with Lessons 1 through 5. They show you the basics on how your PC works and what you need to analyze the components in your PC.

After that feel free to either work through the lessons in order, or jump around from lesson to lesson depending on what you think you need to upgrade. Do whatever *you* need to do to meet your needs.

Helpful Conventions

So that you can move quickly and easily through each lesson, we use a number of standard conventions to help you spot important information. For example:

- Text that will appear on your computer screen appears in **bold** type.

- Buttons, icons, menu items, and such, that you select (and keyboard commands that you press) will appear in color type.

- Information that you are supposed to type appears in **bold color** type.

Additionally, you'll find other important information set off from the main text in boxes like these:

 Plain English   New or technical terms are explained in these boxes, with no jargon allowed, of course.

 Timesaver Tips   Boxes like this will highlight shortcuts and other quick ways to get the job done.

 Panic Button   These boxes caution you about commonly made mistakes or solutions to common problems.

ABOUT THE AUTHOR

Galen A. Grimes has been working with computers since 1980 when he purchased his first PC, an Apple II+. Since then he has worked on PCs using DOS, Windows (3.1/95/NT 4.0), and UNIX, and has programmed in about a dozen different programming languages including C/C++, Assembler, Pascal, BASIC, and xBase. Galen has a master's degree in Information Science from the University of Pittsburgh and is currently a computer systems project manager at Mellon Bank in Pittsburgh, PA.

Galen has worked as an author for several Macmillan Computer Publishing divisions for the past six years and has written *Teach Yourself Netscape Communicator in 24 Hours, 10 Minute Guide to Netscape With Windows 95, 10 Minute Guide to the Internet With Windows 95, 10 Minute Guide to Novell NetWare, 10 Minute Guide to Lotus Improv, First Book of DR DOS 6*, and the best-sellers *10 Minute Guide to the Internet and World Wide Web, 2nd & 3rd Editions*.

Galen co-authored *10 Minute Guide to Netscape Communicator* and *Windows 3.1 Hyperguide*. Galen has also been a contributing author to *Special Edition Using Netscape 2, Special Edition Using CGI, Special Edition Using the World Wide Web, Special Edition Using Netscape 3, Netscape Navigator 3 Starter Kit, WWW Plug-ins Companion, Special Edition Using Netscape Communicator*, and *Internet Starter Kit*.

Although originally born and raised in Texas, Galen currently resides in a quiet, heavily wooded section of Monroeville, PA, a suburb of Pittsburgh, with his wife Joanne. Besides working with computers and surfing the Internet, Galen also spends his time playing golf, bicycling, dabbling in amateur astronomy, gardening, and cooking. Galen can be reached either by email at **gagrimes@city-net.com** or through his web site at **http://www.city-net.com/~gagrimes.**

TRADEMARKS

All terms mentioned in this book that are known to be trademarks have been appropriately capitalized. Sams cannot attest to the accuracy of this information. Use of a term in this book should not be regarded as affecting the validity of any trademark or service mark.

WE'D LIKE TO HEAR FROM YOU!

Sams Publishing has a long-standing reputation for high-quality books and products. To ensure your continued satisfaction, we also understand the importance of customer service and support.

TECH SUPPORT

If you need assistance with the information in this book, please access Macmillan Computer Publishing's online Knowledge Base at **http://www.superlibrary.com/general/support**. If you do not find the answer to your questions on our Web site, you may contact Macmillan Technical Support by phone at **317/581-3833** or via email at **support@mcp.com**.

Also be sure to visit Macmillan's Web resource center for all the latest information, enhancements, errata, downloads, and more. It's located at **http://www.mcp.com/**.

ORDERS, CATALOGS, AND CUSTOMER SERVICE

To order other Sams or Macmillan Computer Publishing books, catalogs, or products, please contact our Customer Service Department at **800/858-7674** or fax us at **800/835-3202** (International Fax: 317/228-4400). Or visit our online bookstore at **http://www.mcp.com/**.

COMMENTS AND SUGGESTIONS

We want you to let us know what you like or dislike most about this book or other Sams products. Your comments will help us to continue publishing the best books available on computer topics in today's market.

Please be sure to include the book's title and author as well as your name and phone or fax number. We will carefully review your comments and share them with the author. Please note that due to the high volume of mail we receive, we may not be able to reply to every message.

Thank you for choosing Sams!

DECIDING TO UPGRADE

1

In this lesson, you learn when you should upgrade components in your existing PC and when you should purchase a new PC.

WHEN SHOULD YOU PURCHASE A NEW PC?

Everyone wants the newest, fastest, most powerful computer available, and it seems that almost every week some computer manufacturer tempts us with the introduction of a new "latest and greatest" speed demon PC. Competition among PC vendors is as hot as ever, and this competition has been both a blessing and a curse for computer purchasers. It has been a blessing because the competition continues to drive down the price of new PCs, PC components, and peripherals while continuously offering a wide selection of new PC models to choose from. The curse side of the competition coin is that with new, faster, and more power-ful PCs always rolling down the assembly line, consumers are forever playing the "wait-for-the-next-model" game—if I wait for the next model, I can get a faster PC with more features.

Rather than wait for the next model, or because they lack the money for a new computer, many users are instead opting to selectively upgrade certain components in their PCs. While up-grading will never give you performance comparable to a new PC, upgrading does have the advantage of allowing you to selec-tively boost your PC's performance and keep your expenses to a minimum.

If you have a PC that's more than four years old, you have to be asking yourself whether you should upgrade or just bite the bullet and buy a new PC. If your old PC is vintage 386 or older, the only question you really have to ask yourself is whether you want a planter or a new boat anchor? Don't waste your time, money, or sanity trying to upgrade a 386 (or God forbid, something older). So many advancements have been made in computer design since the last 386 was boxed up and shipped out—even if you could still find the parts to upgrade a 386-based computer (to something above a 386), the performance would be nothing short of disappointing. Look at it this way; if you are still using a 386, you have long since recouped your initial investment and you have more than gotten your money's worth out of the aging computer. If the message still hasn't reached all remaining 386 owners, let me say it as clearly and succinctly as I can—your computer is obsolete!

However, if you are the owner of an older 486 computer, you have to assess how you are currently using your PC and how to envision using it in the future. If you are still running Microsoft Windows 3.1 on top of some version of MS-DOS (presumably 6.2x) or PC-DOS and you are happy doing a little word processing, email, and occasionally browsing the web on the Internet, then this book will definitely offer you some advice on how you can tweak your system to squeeze just a little bit more performance out of it.

 Using Windows 3.1?   If you are still using Windows 3.1 on your PC, be it a 486 or something newer, make sure you are using at least MS-DOS 6.2x or PC-DOS 7.0. These latest versions of DOS offer you the best memory management possible when working with Windows.

But if you are nursing an aging 486 and you want to step up to one of the 32-bit operating systems offered by Microsoft, such as Windows 95 (see Figure 1.1), the not-yet-released Windows 98, Windows NT 4.0 (see Figure 1.2), or Windows NT 5.0, you likely will not be satisfied with the performance of an upgraded 486. You should also seriously consider purchasing a new computer.

16-bit and **32-bit**   These are technical terms you will hear whenever the discussion turns to operating systems or programming, among other things. Quite simply they refer to how computer instructions and data are processed by your computer—either in 16-bit units or 32-bit units. Because a 32-bit unit is twice as large as a 16-bit unit, the assumption is that 32-bit programs and operating systems are twice as fast as their 16-bit counterparts. Twice as fast may be stretching it a bit, but the basic underlying assumption is generally true—32-bit programs and operating systems are faster than 16-bit programs and operating systems.

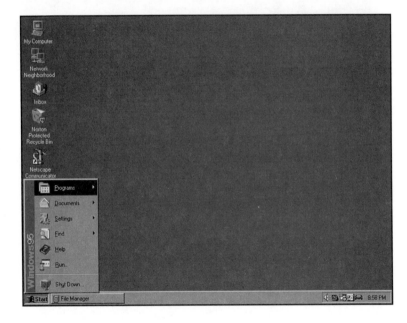

FIGURE 1.1   Windows 95 will run on a 486 or upgrade, but the performance will be marginal.

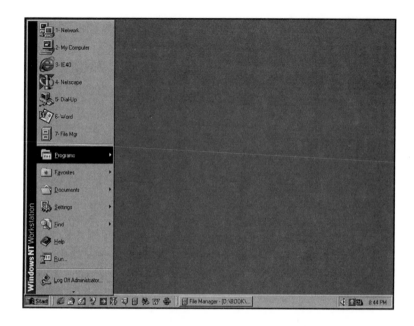

FIGURE 1.2   You will not be satisfied with the performance of Windows NT 4.0 on a 486 or upgrade.

If you have a Pentium-class (Pentium, Pentium Pro, or Pentium II CPU) computer or better, then you should concentrate on examining and upgrading those components in your computer that might be adversely affecting your PC's performance. If you are not sure which components in your computer might be adversely affecting its performance, by the time you complete this book you will know for sure.

In a class by itself   Pentium-class computers are computers equipped with either a Pentium, Pentium Pro, or Pentium II CPU. These are all microprocessors that have been manufactured in the last two years and constitute the current high-end of Intel Corporation's microprocessor line.

WHAT CAN YOU UPGRADE IN YOUR PC?

If you've browsed the Table of Contents, then you already have an idea which components in your PC are upgradable. If you haven't taken a quick look over the TOC, then you may be surprised to learn that almost every component in your PC—including the processor, memory, video card, disk drives, and so on—are candidates to be upgraded.

Which components you decide to upgrade will often be determined by how you use your PC, but not always. Some upgrades make sense to perform simply because the price of the particular component is too good to pass up. In the last two years, the price of memory and hard disk drives have dropped dramatically. I regularly see 32MB of memory priced under $100 and 3GB or more hard disk drives for around $200.

UPGRADING YOUR MEMORY (RAM)

Your PC's memory typically is one of the easiest and least expensive components to upgrade (see Figure 1.3). Upgrading your PC's memory also has the added advantage of improving its performance. Sometimes the improvement in performance is large and other times it is small, but there is always an increase of some type in performance.

 RAM and **memory**   These terms are often used interchangeably. RAM is short for Random Access Memory and is the electronic memory (chips) that your computer uses for running programs and storing temporary data.

FIGURE 1.3   Memory being installed in a PC.

 Performance improvement not noticeable?   Not all
memory performance improvements are readily apparent.
For example, if you boost the memory above 16MB in a
PC running Windows 3.1, the performance improvements
will not be readily apparent because Windows 3.1 cannot
directly access more than 16MB of memory. But the extra
memory can be utilized for disk caching by the
SmartDrive disk cache utility or used to create a RAM
drive to improve the performance of Windows' swap file.
In case the terms are unfamiliar to you, a disk cache is a
temporary holding area in memory for data that your computer might need to quickly access. A swap file is an area
on your hard disk that Windows uses like memory when
all of your RAM (electronic memory) is used up.

Memory upgrades will be covered and explained in detail in
Lesson 6.

UPGRADING YOUR PROCESSOR

Because your processor is largely responsible for how fast your PC and your programs run, upgrading your processor will generally make things run faster. But keep in mind that if you replace the 486 processor in your PC with a 100 MHz Pentium processor, your computer will not operate as fast as a PC built as a 100 MHz Pentium computer because it is not just the processor alone that determines how fast your PC operates. The underlying technology between a 486-class computer and a Pentium-class computer are different, and it is these differences that also contribute to the computer's speed and performance.

 MHz The abbreviation for megahertz (millions of hertz per second), this is used as a measurement for the oscillating timing frequency used by processors. In simpler terms it is an indication of the relative speed of a processor.

Upgrading your processor will generally yield some increase in performance. In Lesson 7, I will explain how you can determine if and when it is advisable to upgrade.

UPGRADING YOUR HARD DISK DRIVE

Upgrading your PC's hard disk drive (see Figure 1.4) is probably the second most common upgrade behind memory upgrades largely because of the dramatic drop in hard disk pricing and the increase in available hard disk sizes.

Upgrading a hard disk is also relatively easy. Although adding a larger hard disk drive might not seem like a significant perfor-mance improvement, consider your own habits in file creation and how often you acquire new programs you would like to try—especially if you regularly download shareware programs from the Internet. If you once had or currently have a small hard disk, (small being defined as any hard disk smaller than 1GB), and you regularly find yourself deleting files to make room for new files or programs, then you can appreciate the performance improvement offered by the addition of a larger hard disk.

FIGURE **1.4**　A new hard disk drive being installed in a PC.

UPGRADING YOUR VIDEO SYSTEM

The majority of the time you choose to upgrade your video system will be for a specific application. For example, you might need a higher resolution to work with a specific application, such as graphic artistry or CAD (computer-aided design). Many of the newer games require better, faster video systems. Even if you are not a graphic artist or CAD engineer, there are still good reasons to upgrade your video system. In Lessons 14 and 15, I'll explain what these reasons are and what benefits you gain from this type of upgrade.

UPGRADING OTHER PC COMPONENTS

The few components mentioned in this lesson are not the only items in your PC you can upgrade. Besides memory, processors, hard disk drives, and video systems, you can also upgrade your floppy and CD-ROM drives, your PC's sound system, modem, system board, and more. In addition to upgrade information, I will offer you some tips and helpful hints on how to diagnose and repair problems involving your hardware components.

In this lesson, you learned about some of the components you can upgrade and a few of the pros and cons associated with each upgrade. In the next lesson, you learn more about some of the components you can upgrade—specifically how to identify each component in your PC and a little about the tasks each component performs.

2

UNDERSTANDING SYSTEM COMPONENTS

In this lesson, you learn about the major system components in your PC and what task each component performs.

UNDERSTANDING YOUR PC AND LOCATING ITS PARTS

Before you can decide which components in your PC you want or need to upgrade, it helps to be able to physically locate each component in your PC and to have a basic understanding of what task each component performs. After you can locate each component and understand what job each component performs, then you can decide which component or components most affect the type of work you do with your computer. For example, if you are a controller, accountant, or some other type of number cruncher, then you will likely be concerned about having the fastest microprocessor to process numbers as quickly as possible. Likewise, if you are a graphic artist or CAD designer, you will likely want to make sure you have the best video system available (as well as a fast microprocessor because overall system speed also affects video output).

Before you can start replacing the "guts" in your computer, you need a short anatomy lesson.

Precautions to Take Before Operating

You need to exercise certain precautions to make sure that when you begin work on your PC, you do not create problems in your attempts to upgrade or repair your computer.

Although many of these precautions will seem like common sense, nevertheless they are worth repeating. So before you take the cover off your PC, do the following:

1. Unplug your PC before you begin working on it. Sometimes you may be tempted to merely hit the on/off switch instead, but on/off switches have been known to malfunction and stick. There is no substitute for pulling the plug to ensure that there is no power to your system.

2. Ground yourself to release static electricity. This is especially important during the winter months when hot, dry air increases the potential for static electricity. All electronic components in your PC can be damaged and/or destroyed by one good jolt. If you have a grounding wrist strap, attach it to your wrist. Otherwise, touch the metal case of your computer or the metal housing around the power supply to ground yourself. You can also touch a metal radiator pipe if you have one handy in your house or wherever you are working on your PC.

3. Make sure that you have an uncluttered workspace. A large kitchen table is an excellent place to work, and because many kitchens have tile or linoleum floors you are also guarding against static electricity at the same time. Consider spreading a large towel under your PC to catch any small screws that you might drop while working on your computer.

Identifying the Parts of Your PC

Before you begin working on your PC, it helps to be able to identify the basic components you might need or want to upgrade or repair. Think of it this way: Before you would attempt to do any routine maintenance on your car, you would want to be able to identify items like an oil filter, a spark plug, and a radiator.

Desktop Versus Tower

Two main types of full-sized PCs currently are available—desktop models (see Figure 2.1) and towers (see Figure 2.2).

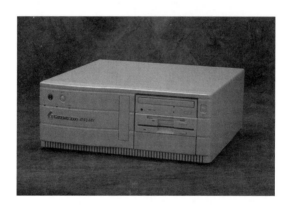

Figure 2.1   A typical desktop PC.

Desktop models may come in several sizes, often called names like "full-size," "baby-AT," or "slim-sized," to denote some difference in relative size, but they all follow the same basic design, which is a PC laid out flat on the desktop.

Tower models also come in a variety of sizes with corresponding names: "mini-tower," "midsize-tower," "full tower," and so on. If you look closely, you can see that a tower is basically just a desktop turned on its side. Turning a desktop on its side to produce a tower model does offer a few advantages. Towers generally take less real estate on your crowded desktop, and larger tower models usually have space for more disk drives.

FIGURE 2.2   A typical tower PC.

EXTERNAL CONNECTIONS

The first things you need to identify are the various external connections on a typical PC. These are usually found on the back of the PC.

Figure 2.3 identifies most of the common external connectors you will find on a typical PC:

- **Serial port.** Used for connecting serial communication devices such as modems, printers, plotters, and so on. Serial ports can be either 9- or 25-pin D-shaped, male connections.

- **Parallel ports.** Used for connecting parallel printers. Parallel ports are 25-pin D-shaped, female connections.

- **VGA video port.** This is what you plug your monitor into, a 15-pin, D-shaped female connector.

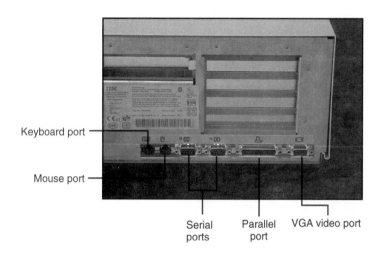

Keyboard port

Mouse port

Serial ports

Parallel port

VGA video port

FIGURE 2.3 The back view of a typical PC.

- **Mouse port.** Your mouse is plugged in here, if you have a mouse port on your PC—some don't and the mouse plugs into a serial port.

- **Keyboard port.** Your keyboard is connected here; there are two types of keyboard connectors—the larger AT-style connector and the smaller PS/2-style connector.

THE MAIN SYSTEM BOARD

After you remove the cover for your PC and look inside, you can see the main system board, also known as the motherboard (see Figure 2.4).

The main system board is usually mounted on the bottom of your PC, if you have a desktop model, or on one side of your PC if you have a tower model. The main system board can be thought of as a connection or communication terminal because many, if not most of the other devices in your PC connect to it, either directly through one of the many connectors built in to the main system board or through an interface card that plugs into the main system board.

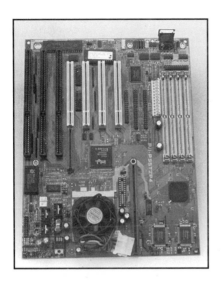

FIGURE 2.4   The main system board inside your PC.

THE MICROPROCESSOR

The microprocessor, also referred to as the CPU or chip, can be plugged into the main system board (see Figure 2.5) and is considered the brains of your PC. The microprocessor executes the instructions that are written into the programs you run on your PC.

FIGURE 2.5   A microprocessor plugged into a main system board.

Can't see your microprocessor? Sometimes your microprocessor is covered by a heat sink. A heat sink is used to help dissipate heat generated by your microprocessor and often looks like a black square or rectangle with a lot of small projections extruding from it.

MEMORY

The memory in your computer is built into modules called SIMMs, which stands for Single Inline Memory Module. SIMMs are electronic modules, about 10-1/2 centimeters long, which sit in slots usually located on your main system board (see Figure 2.6). Even though memory (RAM) and hard disk space are both measured in megabytes (MB) don't confuse the two. Memory is where programs are run, not the space where files are stored.

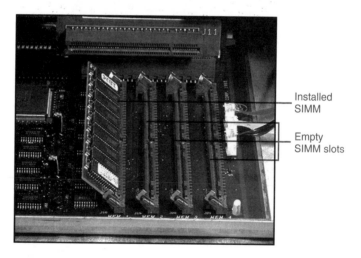

Installed SIMM

Empty SIMM slots

FIGURE 2.6 SIMMs neatly stacked in rows on your main system board.

In some newer computers, SIMMs have been replaced by DIMMs, which stands for Dual Inline Memory Modules. If you compare the two types of memory modules, you see that DIMMs look like over-sized SIMMs.

DISK DRIVES

Most PCs typically have at least two types of disk drives—a single 3 1/2-inch floppy disk drive (see Figure 2.7) and one or more fixed or hard disk drives (see Figure 2.8).

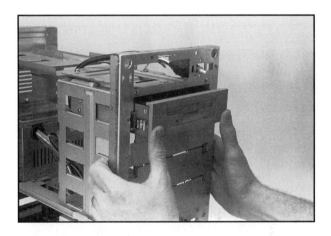

FIGURE 2.7   A 3 1/2-inch floppy disk drive.

INTERFACE CARDS

The final components you need to familiarize yourself with, for now, are your interface cards (see Figure 2.9).

As the name implies, interface cards are used to connect or inter-face your computer to other hardware devices, such as monitors and scanners, or to add additional functionality to your PC in the form of sound cards or modems. Often these are referred to as boards.

FIGURE 2.8   A fixed or hard disk drive.

FIGURE 2.9   Interface cards inserted in the slots on your main system board.

In this lesson, you learned about many of the major components common in most PCs and you also identified which of these major components you have in your computer. In the next lesson, you look a little deeper into your PC and learn how to make your checklist with more than a visual inspection of your PC.

EXAMINING YOUR CURRENT PC

In this lesson, you learn how to take a detailed look at your PC's configuration.

EXAMINING YOUR PC'S CONFIGURATION

In Lesson 2 you looked under the hood of your PC and learned how to identify many of its major components. Now you learn how to delve a bit deeper into your PC and examine its configuration settings. You also will be making a list of the settings as you progress through this lesson. Don't worry if some of the information you encounter seems a bit "techie," arcane, or unnecessary. Even if you don't need all of the information for upgrading purposes, you undoubtedly will need it for problem troubleshooting or when adding new components.

Here is a list of some of the configuration information and settings you learn to check in this lesson:

- Microprocessor (usually referred to as CPU, Central Processing Unit) type and speed

- Amount of memory installed

- Hard disk configuration, including size in megabytes (MB) or gigabytes (GB), average access speed, and throughput

- Floppy disk configuration, including number of floppy drives and size

- Video card manufacturer and amount of video memory installed

- Serial port configuration, including number of ports, interrupts used (including serial ports used by modems)

Interrupts   Most PCs built in the last 10 years or so have a total of 16 interrupts (or Interrupt ReQuests, abbreviated IRQ) numbered 0 through 15. Interrupts are signals various devices use to gain the attention of your CPU when they need processing time. Think of them as the different sounds produced by doorbells at your front and back door. When the doorbell for the front door rings, it means someone at your front door needs your attention, and the differing sounds let you know which door to go to.

- Parallel port configuration

Serial and Parallel ports   Serial ports are also referred to as communication ports, or COM ports. Parallel ports are also referred to as LPT ports, which is short for Line PrinTers, a carryover from computer mainframe days.

In addition to this basic configuration information, you also identify the following:

- If you have a sound card installed and its type
- If you have a CD-ROM drive installed

DIAGNOSTICS AND CONFIGURATION PROGRAMS

Most computers sold in the last few years have been shipped with some type of diagnostics and configuration program capable of providing you with the configuration information mentioned previously. If your computer did not ship with a configuration/

diagnostics program, however, you can download one from the Internet. Watergate Software, Inc. produces a program called PC-Doctor and provides a free evaluation version on its web site. You can download your copy (pcdr15.zip) at **http://www.ws.com/ archives/index.htm** (see Figure 3.1). If you don't have access to the Internet, check with your friends or ask your computer sales-person where you can obtain a copy of this free software.

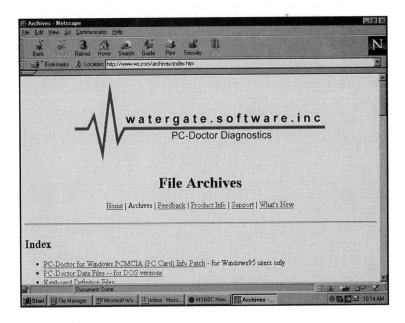

FIGURE 3.1   You can download an evaluation copy of PC-Doctor from the Watergate Software web site.

CREATING YOUR PC-DOCTOR CONFIGURATION DISK

After you download your evaluation copy of PC-Doctor, you need to unzip the file before you can use it.

Unzipping your file   The file you download is in a "zipped" format, meaning that it is in a compressed format to save space and download time. You need a zipfile utility to unzip the file. If you don't already have one, you can download a version of WinZip from **http://www.winzip.com**. Previous versions of WinZip required a second program, Pkunzip. The latest version of WinZip does not require this second program.

To create your configuration disk, follow these steps:

1. Unzip the contents of pcdr15.zip to a floppy disk.

2. Boot your PC by using DOS.

3. Insert your configuration disk and type **pcdr** at the prompt. In a few seconds, PC-Doctor starts (see Figure 3.2).

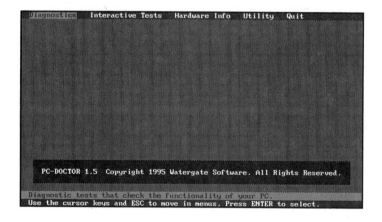

FIGURE 3.2   PC-Doctor's opening screen.

4. From the menu across the top of the screen, select **Hardware Info**.

5. From the Hardware Info menu, select **System Configuration**. In a few seconds PC-Doctor will analyze your PC and display a configuration screen similar to the one you

see in Figure 3.3. Scroll down the page to see all the configuration information PC-Doctor has identified about your PC.

FIGURE 3.3 PC-Doctor's analysis of your PC.

6. To have PC-Doctor identify your interrupt (IRQ) settings, select **IRQ and DMA Use** from the **Hardware Info** menu. In a few seconds, PC-Doctor will display your IRQ settings (see Figure 3.4).

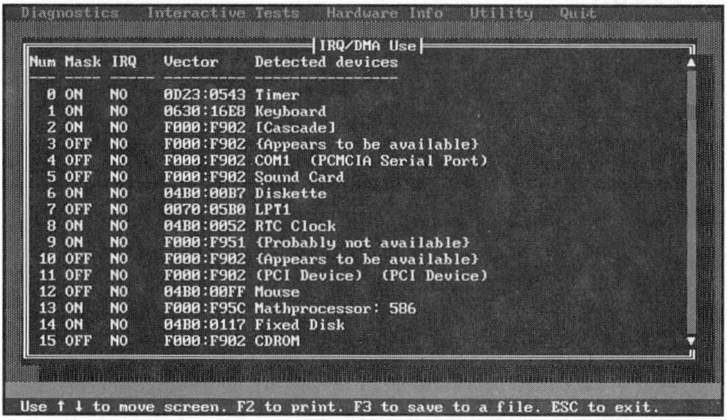

FIGURE 3.4 PC-Doctor displaying the IRQ settings in your PC.

7. You can continue down the Hardware Info menu and have PC-Doctor display the settings for your video configuration (VGA Information), hard disk drives (Physical Disk Drives, Logical Disk Drives, IDE Drive Information), and your serial and parallel ports (COM and LPT ports).

 Print the info   So that you don't have to waste time writing down all of the information PC-Doctor displays about your PC, if you have a printer attached to your computer you can press the F2 key and PC-Doctor will print any configuration screen.

Configuration Information Using Windows 95 and Windows NT 4.0

If you have either Windows 95 or Windows NT 4.0 installed on your computer, you can get the previously listed configuration information without having to resort to the use of a third-party program like PC-Doctor. Both Windows 95 and Windows NT 4.0 include utilities that will display this information about your PC.

Getting Configuration Information Using Windows 95

Windows 95 has a utility in its Control Panel called the Device Manager that you can use to display all the hardware configuration settings for your PC. The only problem you may encounter using the Device Manager is that it displays more information than you necessarily want to know about a particular device, and the information is not always arranged in neat, orderly sections.

To display configuration information about your PC in Windows 95, do the following:

1. Select **Settings** from the **Start** menu, and then open the **Control Panel**. In the Control Panel, double-click the

Systems icon to open the System Properties dialog box. In System Properties, select the **Device Manager** tab to access the Windows 95 Device Manager (see Figure 3.5).

FIGURE 3.5   Shown here is the Windows 95 Device Manager displaying IRQ settings for your PC.

2. Select the **Properties** button near the bottom of the screen; the Device Manager displays the screen listing all the computer's interrupts and which devices they are assigned to.

To Select information about a particular device, perform these steps:

1. Select the particular device you want information about, such as the **Mouse**.

2. If there is a plus sign (+) in front of the device, click it to reveal additional information about that device. In the case of the mouse, the additional information might reveal what type of mouse you have installed if Windows 95 can identify your mouse, or it might just identify your mouse as a Standard PS/2 Port Mouse.

3. Highlight the description of the mouse and then select the **Properties** button to open the properties dialog box about the device you selected. On the first sheet of the

properties dialog box, the Device Manager should display information on whether the device is working properly.

4. Select the **Resources** tab to display the resource information about the mouse and you should see the interrupt (IRQ) the mouse is using (see Figure 3.6).

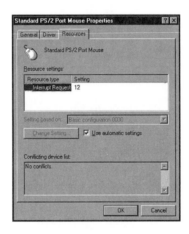

FIGURE 3.6   The Device Manager displays resource information about the mouse.

 Print hardware configuration   The Device Manager can also print the entire hardware configuration for you. At the main Device Manager screen, highlight **Computer** at the top of the device listing and then select the **Print** button.

GETTING CONFIGURATION INFORMATION USING WINDOWS NT 4.0

Windows NT 4.0 includes a program called Windows NT Diagnostics that can display your hardware configuration information much the same as Windows 95's Device Manager.

To start the NT Diagnostics program, follow these steps:

1. From the **Start** menu in NT 4.0, select **Programs**, **Administrative Tools**, and then select **Windows NT Diagnostics** to start the Diagnostics program. In a few seconds the Diagnostics program starts and displays the current version of Windows NT you are running (see Figure 3.7).

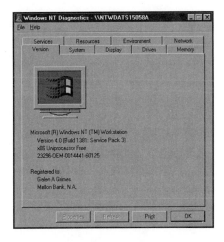

FIGURE 3.7   The Windows NT 4.0 Diagnostics program.

2. After the program starts, you can select the configuration information you want to view by selecting the appropriate tab. For example, to view your video configuration, select the **Display** tab (see Figure 3.8).

3. If you want to view your memory configuration, select the **Memory** tab (see Figure 3.9).

Just like PC-Doctor and the Windows 95 Device Manager, the Windows NT Diagnostics program will make a printout of your hardware configuration.

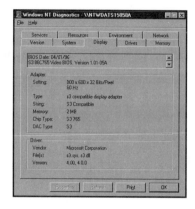

FIGURE 3.8   The Windows NT Diagnostics program displays information on your video configuration.

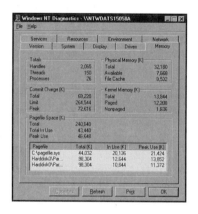

FIGURE 3.9   The Windows NT Diagnostics program displays information on your memory configuration.

In this lesson, you learned how to ferret out the systems details of your hardware configuration regardless of whether you are using DOS, Windows 95, or Windows NT. In the next lesson, you learn about the tools you need to work on your PC.

YOUR CHECKLIST OF TOOLS

In this lesson, you learn what tools you should have on hand for upgrading and repairing your PC and what precautions you should take when working on your PC.

BASIC TOOLS

If you have any experience working on cars or doing simple repairs around the house, you may be surprised to discover that you'll need much fewer tools to work on your PC. After you pop off the cover and start looking around, you'll notice that most of the components are held in place using simple screws, and you'll be able to replace most of the components with either a Phillips (see Figure 4.1) or a medium-sized flat-blade screwdriver (see Figure 4.2).

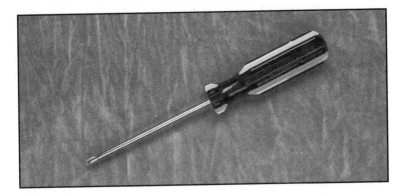

FIGURE 4.1 A typical Phillips-head screwdriver.

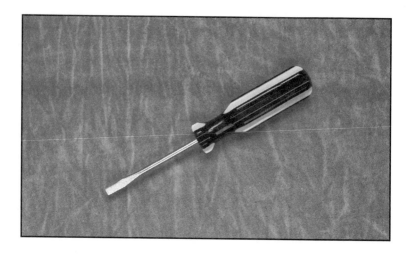

Figure 4.2   A medium-sized flat-blade screwdriver.

You occasionally may run into a few smaller than expected screws and may want to invest $3 or $4 in what are called jeweler's or hobbyist screwdrivers. These are usually sold as a set of six miniature screwdrivers (three Phillips and three flat-blade screwdrivers); you will find these extremely useful if you think you might be doing a lot of work on your PC.

 If you have a Compaq computer   You might find it useful to include a size T15 Torx screwdriver in your toolbox. You find Torx screwdrivers in almost any hardware store. Compaq is the only manufacturer that uses screws requiring a screwdriver other than a Phillips or flat-blade.

Many computer stores also sell computer toolkits with an assortment of PC-related tools (see Figure 4.3), some of which you might find useful and others you might not even be able to figure out what they're for.

FIGURE 4.3   A typical PC toolkit.

One of the most useful tools you will run across in these types of kits is the 3-pronged probe. A 3-pronged probe looks like a metal or plastic syringe with three moveable "fingers" where the syringe needle would normally be found. This is an invaluable tool for retrieving very small screws that you will invariably drop inside your PC. A small pair of needle-nosed pliers or a small pair of surgical forceps, both sold in hobby stores, will work in place of the 3-pronged probe, but you will likely find the probe easier to manipulate.

OTHER USEFUL TOOLS AND ACCESSORIES

Although you may not consider the following items to be tools, nonetheless you will find them extremely useful and should always include them in your toolbox.

The first two items are simple pencil and paper. Whenever you attempt to replace any component in your PC, you should always draw a diagram first, listing exactly where in your PC the component is being removed from and any cables or attachments connected to that component.

 How's it attached? Whenever you remove a cable from a component inside your PC, pay particular attention to the orientation of the cable. Several types of cables in your PC can be attached more than one way.

While you have pencil and paper in hand, you should also get into the habit of keeping a log or journal of all changes you make to your PC. This log should include all changes made to your system as well as components you add. Be sure to include the date the change was made.

The next items you will find extremely helpful when working on your PC are small, self-sticking labels, such as Avery or Brady labels. You should attach a numbered label (numbered 1, 2, 3...) to every wire or cable you remove whenever you are working on your PC and mark on your diagram the corresponding numbered cable and its location. This arrangement will enable you to quickly and easily identify what each wire or cable is attached to.

If you are like most PC users, you might open your PC once or twice a year, if that often. After 6–12 months or longer, you'll find a considerable amount of dust built up in your system. A layer of dust in your PC causes more problems than mere aesthetics. A layer of dust can act as an insulating material trapping heat that otherwise would be dissipated through the normal fan-controlled air circulation system. In short, the more dust you let accumulate in your PC, the quicker it will overheat, and overheating damages your PC.

One of the best solutions for preventing dust build-up is to periodically take the cover off your PC and "blow it out" using compressed air. Compressed air canisters can be purchased from virtually any office supply store for a few dollars and should be part of every PC user's repair and maintenance toolbox.

Rearranged dust If at all possible, take your PC out-doors before you "blow it out." Otherwise you'll end up making a bigger mess by merely shifting the dust from the inside of your PC to the outside of your PC and all over your desk. If you can't take your PC outside, at least move it off your desk and to a room where you can later vacuum the dust you remove.

Safety Precautions You Need to Remember

Whenever you work on your PC, you need to put a number of safety precautions into practice, not only to protect your PC from possible damage, but also to protect yourself from possible harm.

Unplug Your PC

This is the number one safety precaution and cannot be repeated often enough. Either unplug your PC at the wall outlet or from the back of the PC. Don't merely rely on the on/off switch. Be-sides possibly risking a potentially lethal electrical shock to your-self, you can damage your PC and its internal components if you accidentally try to remove a card or other device while it is still receiving current. You could also accidentally drop a screwdriver or other metal tool on your main system board and cause a short.

Ground Yourself

Although not properly grounding yourself for static electricity is much more of a potential threat to your PC than to yourself, don't underestimate this risk, especially during the cold winter months when circulating air in homes and offices tends to be drier than normal. Most of the sensitive electronic components in your PC (microprocessors, memory, interface cards, and so on) can be seriously damaged or even destroyed by stray jolts of static. Make sure you touch a metal object such as a desk, a chair, or a filing cabinet before you begin work on your PC. Also, if possible, move your PC to a room that does not have a carpeted floor—most carpeting used in homes and offices contains synthetic fibers that can increase the potential for static electric discharge.

KEEP MAGNETS AWAY FROM PCs

Static electricity is not the only charge you want to keep away from your PC. Magnetic charges can also damage some PC components, such as disk drives. Make sure that any tools you use are not magnetized (such as screwdrivers).

In this lesson, you learned what tools you need to work on your PC and received a few suggestions on some additional tools and accessories that will help make working on your PC easier. You also learned about safety precautions you need to take to protect yourself and your PC. In the next lesson, you learn how your computer keeps track of its hardware settings.

UNDERSTANDING YOUR CMOS SETTINGS

5

*In this lesson, you learn how your PC
stores its configuration information and how you can
change these configuration settings.*

CMOS MEMORY

Have you ever paid attention to what your computer does every time you turn it on? If you haven't, stop for a moment and go turn on your PC; this time watch closely as your computer starts.

One of the operations your computer performs each time it starts is to read its configuration settings. The settings are read from a special area of memory where they are stored for easy retrieval by your computer. This special area of memory is called *CMOS Memory*. CMOS stands for *Complementary Metal-Oxide Semiconductor*, which is a type of memory that can hold its contents using a very low electrical current. CMOS memory is used to store your computer's configuration information, and its electrical current is supplied by battery backup when your computer is turned off.

It is not just important that your computer be able to access its configuration information—it is critical to its operation. Part of the information read from CMOS memory informs your computer about how your hard disk drive is configured. If this information is missing or incorrect, your hard disk will not function and your computer will not boot.

 Boot A shortened form of "pulling yourself up by your bootstraps." In computer terms this means for the computer to load its operating system (DOS, Windows 95, Windows NT, OS/2) and begin operations.

This lesson is not about warning you of the dire consequences that could befall you every time you turn on your PC. This lesson is intended to teach you how to access the information stored in CMOS memory so that you will have it available if your computer should lose its CMOS contents. This lesson also explains how to make changes in CMOS memory when you make upgrades to your computer.

ACCESSING YOUR CMOS MEMORY

Every computer comes with a program that you can use to access the contents of your computer's CMOS memory. In early computers the program to access CMOS memory was often included on a floppy disk that you needed to run. Nowadays just about every computer has this program built in to the computer so that it is always available for you to use. You may have noticed that when you turned on your computer, one of the messages prompted you to enter a certain key sequence, like Ctrl+Alt+Esc or Ctrl+Alt+S or the F1, F2, or the Del key to run Setup. This Setup program is the utility you run to access your computer's CMOS memory.

Not prompted for Setup?   If you are running an older 486 computer, there's a good chance you will not see any message during startup that prompts you on how to start your computer's Setup program. This means that you must run Setup from a disk included by the compu-ter's manufacturer. If you can't locate the disk with Setup, contact your manufacturer. It's likely the manufacturer has a bulletin board service you can call into or a site on the Internet where you can download a new copy of Setup.

To access the Setup program in your computer, follow these steps:

1. If your computer is currently on, turn it off and then turn it back on.

2. As your computer is starting, watch for any message indicating a particular key—such as F1, F2, or Del—or a key

sequence—such as Ctrl+Alt+Esc or Ctrl+Alt+S—to start your computer's Setup program. If you do not see a message indicating a key sequence for starting Setup, try pressing Ctrl+Alt+Esc or Ctrl+Alt+S to see whether a Setup program starts. If you cannot start Setup using a key sequence, it probably means that your Setup program is not built-in to your computer. In this case, you will need to locate a copy of the Setup program. Checking with the manufacturer of the computer is your best bet for locating the Setup program. Your Setup program may look something like Figure 5.1.

```
                        Phoenix Technologies Ltd.    Version
                        System Configuration Setup    4.03  00
Time     21:04:00
Date     Wed Dec 10,  1997

Diskette A:             3.5 inch, 1.44 MB
Diskette B:             Not Installed Cyl   Hd    Pre   LZ    Sec Size
Hard Disk 1:            Not Installed
Hard Disk 2:            Not Installed
Hard Disk 3:            Not Installed
Hard Disk 4:            Not Installed

HD1 Block Mode :        Disabled        HD2 Block Mode  :  Disabled
HD3 Clock Mode :        Disabled        HD4 Block Mode  :  Disabled

Base Memory:            640 KB
Extended Memory:        19456 KB
Display:                VGA/EGA
IDE Controller Speed:   Medium


PgUp for specific options.  Up/Down arrow to select.  Left/Right arrow
to change.
F1 for Help. F10 to Exit. ESC to reboot.
```

FIGURE 5.1   An example of a typical hardware Setup program.

3. Write down all the information you see on your computer's hardware setup, and keep this information in a safe place. If you should lose the information in your computer's CMOS memory, you will need this information to reenter your CMOS settings. Be careful when you are stepping through your Setup program so that you don't accidentally change any settings. And absolutely, don't start experimenting with

different settings to see what they do. Entering the wrong information here can render your computer unusable and in some cases could actually damage it.

When you actually begin upgrading some of the components in your PC in later lessons, you will be making changes to the settings in your computer's CMOS memory.

In this lesson, you learned how to access the CMOS memory in your computer by using your PC's Setup program. In the next lesson, you learn how to upgrade the memory in your PC.

Upgrading Your PC's Memory

In this lesson, you learn how to upgrade the memory in your PC.

Why You Need More Memory

When you say you are upgrading the memory in your computer, what you are really saying is that you are adding more memory to your computer. Increasing the amount of memory in your PC literally gives you the "most bang for your buck" in terms of the amount of money you spend and the resulting increase in performance you gain. Whereas processor type and speed largely control how fast most operations on your PC are performed, memory is probably the largest factor controlling how many tasks you can perform simultaneously, especially if you are working in one of the Windows environments (3.1, 95, or NT), and how well each task performs.

Although the performance gains are much more pronounced under one of the 32-bit Windows environments (95, NT), boosting your memory from 8MB to 16MB under Windows 3.1 will often produce a dramatic improvement in performance and in the number of Windows applications you can run simultaneously. You really should not consider running Windows 95 with less than 16MB of memory since your performance will suffer. As for Windows NT, the suggested minimum memory will vary depending on whom you talk to, but most experts say around 16–24MB.

Memory—MB and KB Let's clarify another potential problem area. If you have 8MB, 16MB, or 32MB (or however much you have installed) of memory installed in your PC, this amount is expressed as 8,192, or 16,384, or 32,768 instead of 8,000 or 16,000 or 32,000. The reason is because a megabyte of memory is actually 1,024KB rather than 1,000KB of memory. Remember that computers are binary (using 0s and 1s) devices. 1,024 is simply 2^{10}, which is close enough to 1,000 to be a workable unit of measurement.

HOW MEMORY WORKS IN YOUR PC

Random Access Memory (RAM, or merely shortened to simply memory) is used as a storage area for your microprocessor (also called your Central Processing Unit or CPU) for calculations, data, and the programs currently being run. Information remains in RAM only while the PC's power is on, which is why you have to save to disk any files you are working on before you turn the power off (and why you lose work if the power accidentally goes out).

WHAT TYPE OF MEMORY DO YOU NEED?

The answer to this question is simple—you add the same type of memory you are currently using in your PC. The sections that follow list memory types used in 486 and Pentium-based computers (remember we said in Lesson 1 that if you have a 386 PC, don't bother upgrading—get a new computer).

MEMORY FOR 486 COMPUTERS

Memory used in 486-based computers are installed in modules called SIMMs—Single Inline Memory Modules. Basically two types of SIMMs are used in 486 computers: 72-pin SIMMs and 30-pin SIMMs (see Figure 6.1).

FIGURE 6.1   72-pin SIMMs and 30-pin SIMMs.

In older 486 computers using 30-pin SIMMs, the SIMMs were usually housed in groups of 4 or 8. 30-pin SIMMs were manufactured as 256K and 1MB SIMMs. Some computers using 30-pin SIMMs did allow you to mix 256K and 1MB SIMMs in the same computer. If you are upgrading a PC that uses 30-pin SIMMs, you should remove any 256K SIMMs you might have and replace them with 1MB SIMMs. This will give you a maximum of 8MB of RAM in your PC. Be sure to check your PC manual for the appropriate combinations of SIMMs you can install in your PC.

Later model 486 computers use 72-pin SIMMs. 72-pin SIMMs are available in sizes of 1MB, 4MB, 8MB, 16MB, and 32MB. The main considerations for using 72-pin SIMMs are:

- The size (4MB, 8MB, and so on) your main system board will support

- Whether your main system board uses parity SIMMs or no-parity SIMMs

Parity chip   In older 72-pin SIMMs, an additional memory chip was installed—a parity chip, which was used for error-checking the data held in memory. As the quality of memory making improved, the parity "error-checking" chip was no longer needed, though some manufacturers still include them. Non-parity SIMMs sometimes are priced slightly lower than parity SIMMs.

- The speed, as measured in nanoseconds (ns), of the SIMM—most 72-pin SIMMs used in 486 computers were 70 ns, whereas Pentium-based SIMMs were 60 ns

Matching parity   If you are upgrading a 486 computer, SIMM parity and speed are important because you need to match the memory currently installed in your PC. Matching speed is not as critical as matching parity because mismatched speed in SIMMs will just cause your computer to operate at the slowest speed installed. Matching parity is critical because a mismatch in parity will cause your PC to fail.

MEMORY FOR PENTIUMS

Early model computers using the Pentium processor used 72-pin SIMMs, but later model Pentiums were manufactured to use DIMMs (Dual Inline Memory Modules). If you hold a SIMM and a DIMM next to each other, the DIMM looks like a very large SIMM.

In 486-based computers you could install a single SIMM, but Pentium-based computers require you to install SIMMs in pairs. Because DIMMs are the electronic equivalent of 2 SIMMs, you can install a single DIMM in a Pentium-based (including Pentium Pros and Pentium IIs) computer instead of a pair of SIMMs.

In all cases, whether you are adding memory to a 486 or Pentium computer, check your computer's documentation first. If you cannot locate the documentation or if it does not specify the type of memory you should use, check with the manufacturer of the computer. In some cases you can simply specify what type of computer you have (manufacturer and model) when ordering memory, and the company you are ordering from can determine what type of memory you need.

INSTALLING MEMORY IN YOUR PC

Make sure that you exercise the safety precautions detailed in Lessons 3 and 4 before you begin. It is especially important that you shutdown and unplug your computer before beginning this task. Also, make sure that you keep your SIMMs or DIMMs in the anti-static containers until you are ready to install them. Just as static electricity can damage the components in your computer, static electricity can also damage computer memory.

INSTALLING SIMMs

Before you begin, look closely at how your SIMMs are installed in your computer. At each end of the SIMM is a small clip holding the SIMM in place. Notice too that the ends of the SIMMs are not the same. One end of your SIMM is square and the other end looks like it has a small rounded notch removed. When you insert a new SIMM in your computer, make sure that you align the squared end and the notched end the same as your existing SIMMs. You will also notice, printed on your main system board, that the SIMM slots are numbered, usually 0 through 3 or 0 through 7. Always fill the lowest numbered empty slot. For example, if you have SIMMs installed in slots 0 and 1, the next SIMM would be installed in slot 2.

To install memory SIMMs in your computer, follow these steps:

1. Hold the SIMM by the top edge and gently insert the SIMM into an empty SIMM slot at an angle (see Figure 6.2).

FIGURE 6.2   Inserting a new SIMM into an empty SIMM slot.

2. Apply even pressure on the SIMM and gently push the top edge of the SIMM down so that the new SIMM is inserted into the slot at the same angle as the existing SIMMs (see Figure 6.3). You should hear a slight snap as the SIMM clips grasp the newly inserted SIMM. If your clips are plastic, be very careful not to accidentally break the clips.

 Note that many SIMMs will mount fully upright (or perpendicular to the motherboard) and not angled, as shown in Figure 6.3. Take note of how the original SIMMs appeared when installed and make sure that you install the new SIMMs in the same manner.

FIGURE 6.3   A newly inserted SIMM in a SIMM slot is shown here.

Depending on the computer you have, your PC may work with the newly installed memory without any further action on your part. However, some computers will report a memory error and force you to run your computer's hardware Setup program (see Lesson 5) to adjust the value for the amount of memory installed. Essentially, you are changing the amount of memory from the amount you had before you installed the additional SIMM(s) to the amount of memory now installed in your PC. After you make the adjustment, be sure to save the changes you make and then reboot your PC. Your PC should now recognize the memory you installed and make the memory available for use by your programs.

INSTALLING DIMMs

DIMMs are actually easier to install than SIMMs. DIMMs install in slots similar to SIMMs except that DIMMs are not angled in the slots. DIMMs insert straight down into the slots. And unlike the clips for SIMMs, when the DIMM is inserted, the pressure of the DIMM forces the clips to fold inward, holding the DIMM in place.

ADDING MEMORY WHEN YOUR SOCKETS ARE FULL

One problem you are likely to run into sooner or later is wanting to add additional memory to your PC but having no empty SIMM sockets in which to add SIMMs. There are two solutions:

- Remove your old SIMMs and replace them with larger SIMMs.

- Buy a SIMM adapter.

A SIMM adapter is a device that allows you to insert up to four SIMMs into one SIMM socket (see Figure 6.4).

FIGURE 6.4   A SIMM adapter supporting four SIMMs in one socket.

SIMM adapters come in a myriad of configurations and can be used to:

- Adapt 30-pin SIMMs into a 72-pin socket

- Adapt 72-pin SIMMs into a 30-pin socket

- Adapt multiple 72-pin SIMMs into a single 72-pin socket

When you purchase a SIMM adapter, you need to do some careful planning beforehand. You need to plan what type of SIMMs you want to use in the adapter and which way the SIMMs and the adapter will be facing in the socket so that the adapter will not be blocking other SIMM sockets or blocking other devices in your computer. You can find out more about SIMM adapters at **http://www.tsicorp.com/**.

In this lesson, you learned how to upgrade the memory in your PC. In the next lesson, you learn how to upgrade your PC's microprocessor.

PROCESSOR UPGRADES

In this lesson, you learn how to upgrade your central processing unit.

UNDERSTANDING PROCESSORS

The heart of your computer is the processor. The processor is also referred to as the microprocessor or the central processing unit (or CPU). Whatever name you prefer, they all refer to the chip inside your computer that processes instructions. Most PCs contain processors made by Intel Corporation (as in the "Intel Inside" commercials you've undoubtedly seen on television), but some PCs contain processors made by Digital, Motorola, AMD, and Cyrix.

 Multimedia included   One other buzzword you will be hearing a lot now is MMX. MMX refers to a set of instructions Intel has placed inside its latest Pentium processor. The new instructions pertain to multimedia (MMX stands for Multi Media eXtensions) and make it easier and a lot faster for the new processor to work with graphics, animation, sound, and so on. These multimedia instructions are now a part of the processor rather than instructions received through software.

UPGRADE CONSIDERATIONS

If and when you decide to upgrade your processor, you must consider a few other factors. These factors relate to your computer and how upgradeable your PC is designed to be. The main three factors you have to consider are:

- **Clock speed**. What is the clock speed (measured in megahertz) of your current processor? This is simply a measurement of your current processor's speed. There is much debate about how much of an improvement in clock speed you should upgrade to. Some people use the "100% rule," which means that a new processor should be at least 100 percent faster than your current processor. For example, if your current processor is a 50 MHz model, any upgrade you consider should at least be a 100 MHz processor or faster. Even if you cannot follow the 100% rule, any faster processor in your PC will improve your computer's performance. The 100% rule is a rough guarantee that the level of performance will be worth your investment.

- **Bus speed and width**. Your PC's bus is a pipeline that transports data to and from the processor to the other components and peripherals in your computer, such as memory, disk drives, interface cards, and so on. Your processor speed is largely irrelevant if you have a slow bus or if you have a 64-bit processor (Pentium) and a 32-bit (486) wide bus.

 Bus speed   This refers to how fast information and instructions can travel between your processor and the peripherals in your computer the processor must communicate with, such as your hard drives, memory, interface cards, and so forth.

- **Computer expansion options**. A way of upgrading your processor. Some early processors were soldered onto the main system board, making them impossible to remove without destroying your system board. Make sure that your PC has an empty socket for another processor, or make sure your current processor can be removed and replaced by a newer, faster processor.

IDENTIFYING YOUR CPU

If you've decided to take the plunge and upgrade your processor, you first need to locate and identify the CPU currently in your PC. After you take the cover off (make sure you exercise all cautions mentioned in Lessons 3 and 4), look for what is probably the largest chip in your computer. On many computers the processor will be in a plastic holder called a *ZIF* socket (see Figure 7.1).

 ZIF   Stands for *Zero Insertion Force*. One common problem in inserting chips is the possibility of bending or breaking the pins when you press (or jam) the pins of the chip into very tight socket holes. In a ZIF socket, you don't have to press the pins of the chip into a socket. Instead you merely place the pins into oversized socket holes and move a lever that grabs the pins and holds the chip in the socket.

The CPU   The ZIF socket

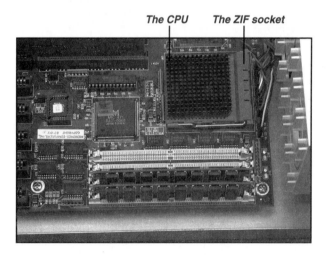

FIGURE 7.1   CPU in a ZIF socket.

My CPU is stuck If you discover that your CPU is soldered to your main system board, replace the cover and forget upgrading. If you want a faster PC, you will have to purchase a newer PC or replace the main system board (see Lesson 8, "Replacing Your System Board").

Don't be surprised if you remove the cover and don't see anything that looks like a CPU. On some smaller systems, it's not uncommon to have disk drive housings covering your CPU. If this is the case, then you will have to also remove your disk drives (see Lesson 9, "Hard Disk Upgrades" and Lesson 10, "Replacing a Floppy Disk Drive,") to get to your CPU. Just pay careful attention to anything you remove (make a diagram if it will help you remember), and be sure to replace any components exactly the same way you removed them.

After you've located your processor, the first thing you need to look for is any writing on the CPU identifying what type it is. Figure 7.2 shows you what to look for. You will be looking for information identifying the CPU as a 486 or Pentium and information displaying its speed.

Figure 7.2 An Intel CPU displaying its type and speed.

If the CPU info is covered Some processors will be covered by a heat sink or a fan. A heat sink looks like several dozen long slender projectiles sticking out of your processor. These are used to help dissipate the heat that processors give off. If you can't see anything identifying the processor type and speed, go back to Lesson 3 and pull out one of the utilities you used to identify your PC components.

You need to know exactly the type of processor installed in your PC in order to purchase an upgrade. Besides making sure you purchase a faster upgrade processor, you also need to know what type of processor is currently installed to make sure you purchase an upgrade that is compatible with your computer system. Besides speed, slight voltage differences also exist between some processors. If you know exactly what type of processor is currently installed in your PC, when you are ready to purchase an upgrade processor the company you purchase the upgrade from will be able to sell you an upgrade processor guaranteed to operate correctly in your PC.

SELECTING AN UPGRADE PROCESSOR

Even if your PC has a processor made by Intel, you might want to consider upgrading to a CPU manufactured by AMD or Cyrix because of certain limitations on Intel's upgrade path. For example, if you currently have an early model Intel Pentium processor, such as a 75 MHz model, you cannot upgrade that CPU to an Intel Pentium Pro 180 or 200 MHz model, or an Intel Pentium II 233 or 266 MHz processor because the newer Pentium processors will not fit into the socket of the original Pentium processor. You can replace your Intel Pentium 75MHz CPU with a 233 MHz model K6 chip from AMD, however, because the AMD K6 chip will fit into the socket used by the Intel 75 MHz Pentium processor. There are also models of the Cyrix CPUs that are a pin-for-pin replacement of earlier model Intel Pentium chips.

Check out AMD or Cyrix   You can check whether AMD and Cyrix CPUs can be used as replacements for your existing Intel CPU by checking information on AMD's (**http://www.amd.com**) and Cyrix's (**http://www.cyrix.com**) web sites.

REMOVING THE CPU

If your main system board (your motherboard) is equipped with a ZIF socket, removing the current processor will be a snap. To remove a processor from a ZIF socket, follow these steps:

1. Swing back the ZIF socket lever to release tension on the pins.

2. Gently lift out the processor.

If your motherboard does not have a ZIF socket, you can still remove your processor with a minimal amount of effort. Many companies that sell upgrade processors include a processor extraction tool with the upgrade. The extraction tool looks like a small crowbar or prybar except that it is wider and has a few more teeth. To remove the processor using the extraction tool, do the following:

1. Gently insert the extraction tool under each of the four sides of the processor, and gently press down on the extraction tool. The tool is designed so that this downward pressure will lift up on the processor.

2. Repeat step 1 as many times as necessary until you can gently lift the processor out of the socket.

Invest in an Extraction tool If your upgrade processor is not shipped with an extraction tool, run down to the local computer store and purchase one. The tool will cost you only a dollar or two and is well worth the investment because it will (almost) guarantee that you will safely remove the processor without damaging it or your motherboard.

As you remove your old processor, note that one corner of the processor is notched (see Figure 7.3).

Notice that the notched corners line up.

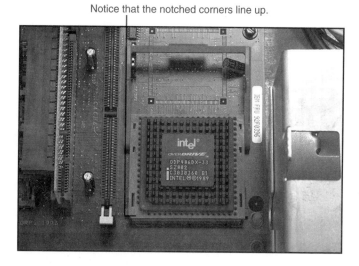

FIGURE 7.3   Each CPU has a notched corner to properly line up the CPU with the socket.

Notice that the notched corner of the processor is lined up with a similarly notched corner of the socket. When you insert the upgrade processor, you must make sure that the notches line up exactly as they do with the old processor.

Line up the notches   If the notch on the upgrade processor is not lined up exactly with the notch on the socket, your PC will not operate correctly and you could damage the upgrade processor.

INSERTING THE NEW CPU

Make sure that you are grounded before you remove the upgrade processor from its container. Ground yourself by touching a metal object like the housing around your PC's power supply or if a metal pipe is handy in your house. To insert the upgrade processor in your PC, follow these steps:

1. Locate the notch on your upgrade processor and on the processor socket.

2. Line up the notches and carefully insert the upgrade processor into the socket. If you have a ZIF socket, simply move the locking lever back to the lock position. If you do not have a ZIF socket, gently apply pressure to the center of the processor until it is firmly seated in the socket.

On many PCs your new processor should be recognized and configured automatically to operate in your PC. If your PC displays an error message when turned on, run your computer's hardware Setup program as you did in Lesson 5 to configure your PC with your upgrade processor. Check your manual, too, to see if any jumpers on your motherboard need to be changed or set when you install a new processor.

In this lesson, you learned how to select and install an upgrade processor in your PC. In the next lesson, you learn how to select and install a new main system board in your PC.

REPLACING YOUR SYSTEM BOARD

In this lesson, you learn how to replace the main system board in your PC.

ARE YOU UPGRADING OR REPLACING?

The majority of the time main system boards are replaced in PCs, the board is replaced with a similar or comparable model as opposed to having the board upgraded to a more advanced model. As you might guess, the determining factors here are cost versus performance. If you purchase a system board that offers a significant level of performance above the board you are replacing, you will most likely also have to replace additional components in your PC, such as the processor, memory, and often the interface cards as well. By the time you add up this additional expense, it probably wouldn't cost you much more to purchase a new PC.

In Lesson 7, one of the factors you were told to consider in deciding whether you wanted to upgrade your processor was bus speed.

Bus speed   The bus in your PC is the connecting pipeline between your processor, memory, and the PC's peripherals, such as drives and interface cards. Bus speed refers to how fast data and instructions are able to move between the CPU, memory, and your PC's peripherals. Part of bus speed is controlled by how wide the bus is. Width refers to how much data can be passed at one time—8 bits of data, 16 bits of data, or 32 bits of data. Obviously, a bus that can pass data 32 bits at a time can operate faster than a bus that can pass data only 8 bits at a time. To use an analogy, think of a water pipe that is 1 inch in diameter versus a water pipe 4 inches in diameter. The 4-inch pipe allows more water to pass every second than does the 1-inch pipe.

In the past few years, PC buses haven't just gotten faster, PC buses have also changed in terms of physical design. Bus design not only affects the speed and performance of your PC, but bus design also affects the type of interface cards you can use in your PC.

The "IBM PC" or PC-compatible computer has seen six major bus designs:

- **8-bit ISA (or "original IBM-PC") bus**. The original 8-bit bus design used in IBM PCs, XTs, and early PC-compatible computers.

- **16-bit ISA bus**. The first 16-bit bus was essentially a 16-bit upgrade of the original IBM PC bus; the ISA bus was used originally in the IBM-AT computer and AT-compatible computers.

- **Micro Channel Architecture (MCA) bus**. IBM's proprietary 32-bit bus, used in its PS/2 computer line. No manufacturer but IBM ever used this bus design because other manufacturers did not want to pay license fees to IBM.

- **EISA bus**. The computer industry's response to IBM's proprietary MCA bus; used mainly in network file servers manufactured by Compaq.

- **VESA Local bus**. The first 32-bit bus design used in 486 computers that was fast enough to support graphical environments.

- **PCI bus**. Designed to overcome many of the speed limitations of the VESA local bus to support the higher bus speeds required by the Pentium processor line.

If you are using a 486 computer or faster, you only have to be concerned with the last two bus designs—the VESA local bus (also called VL-bus) and the PCI bus. You can easily tell the difference between a VESA local bus motherboard and a PCI bus motherboard merely by looking at them. Each use a distinctive slot design for either VESA or PCI bus interface cards. Figure 8.1 displays a VESA bus motherboard and Figure 8.2 shows a PCI motherboard.

VESA bus slot

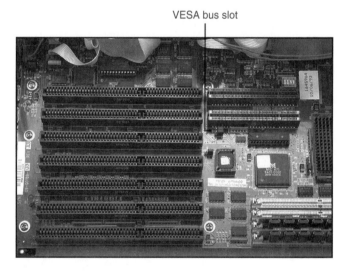

FIGURE 8.1   A VESA local bus motherboard.

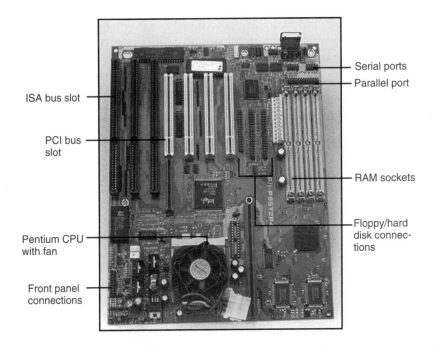

ISA bus slot

PCI bus slot

Pentium CPU with fan

Front panel connections

Serial ports

Parallel port

RAM sockets

Floppy/hard disk connections

FIGURE 8.2   A PCI bus motherboard.

Notice that both motherboards still include a number of ISA slots for older interface cards. Notice, too, that neither motherboard has slots for the other type of motherboard—a VESA local bus motherboard does not have PCI slots and a PCI bus motherboard does not have VESA local bus slots. Regardless of which mother- board design you have, you most likely have, at the very least, a video interface card and maybe one or more other interface cards designed specifically for that type of bus slot.

By now you should at least start to see the problems of converting your PC from one bus type motherboard to the other. If you have a PCI bus motherboard, converting it to a VESA local bus would be a step backward because the VESA local bus design is an older and slower type bus than the PCI type bus. It is also next to im- possible to still find VESA bus-type interface cards, even at com- puter shows. And if you have a VESA local bus-type motherboard, converting to a PCI bus-type motherboard would entail replacing all of your VESA bus-type interface cards. Another factor to consider is that in many cases memory used in VESA local bus-type mother- boards is slower than memory used in PCI type motherboards.

SELECTING A REPLACEMENT MOTHERBOARD

When you select a replacement motherboard, there is a bit more than merely selecting the same type motherboard as is currently installed in your computer. The same type motherboards often come in different sizes so it is important to select a motherboard that will fit in your existing computer case.

MOTHERBOARD SIZES AND TYPES

After you've identified the type of system board in your computer (VESA local bus or PCI), you need to identify the size system board used in your computer. Motherboards come in five basic sizes—standard AT, baby AT, LPX, ATX, and NLX.

STANDARD AT SIZE

The standard AT size motherboard is the largest motherboard still available. The system board is so named because it is about the same size as the motherboard used in the original IBM AT com- puter. These boards can be up to 12 inches wide by 13.8 inches long.

THE BABY AT SIZE MOTHERBOARD

The Baby AT size motherboard is just a smaller version of the standard AT size motherboard. This motherboard is smaller be- cause it uses newer technology that allows manufacturers to min- iaturize many of the components used on the standard AT size motherboard. Figure 8.3 shows a standard AT size motherboard on the left and a baby AT motherboard on the right.

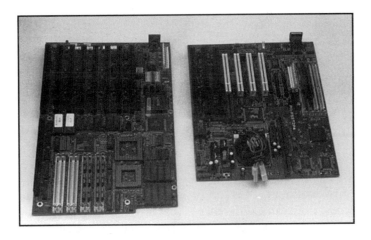

FIGURE **8.3**   Standard AT motherboard and baby AT motherboard.

THE **LPX** AND MINI-**LPX** MOTHERBOARDS

The LPX and mini-LPX motherboards are easily identified by a unique physical characteristic not present in either the AT or baby AT motherboards—a "riser" card into which interface cards are connected. This model was originally developed by Western Digital and is still being used by IBM, Compaq, and Gateway, among others (see Figure 8.4).

FIGURE **8.4**   An LPX style motherboard with a riser card.

LPX motherboard limitations Two problems with LPX motherboards are they have limited expandability because they generally have fewer expansion slots, and it is difficult to obtain an LPX motherboard (usually) except from the manufacturer. Manufacturers generally charge more than computer stores for replacement motherboards.

THE ATX MOTHERBOARD

The ATX motherboard is sort of a hybrid baby AT motherboard. The most noticeable difference is that layout of components on the board appears to have been shifted sideways (see Figure 8.5). This is the design being used in most newer computers. You should be aware that ATX motherboards will not fit in cases designed for either the mini-LPX or the LPX motherboards.

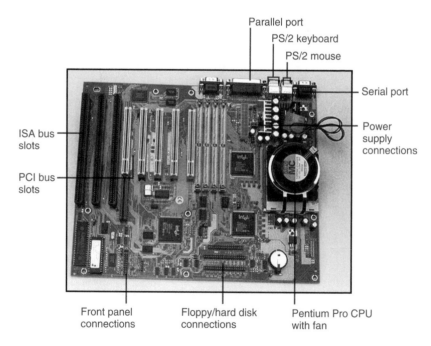

FIGURE 8.5   An ATX motherboard.

THE NLX MOTHERBOARD

The NLX style motherboard is designed specifically for the Pentium II processor and it uses many of the best design features of both the ATX and LPX style motherboards (see Figure 8.6).

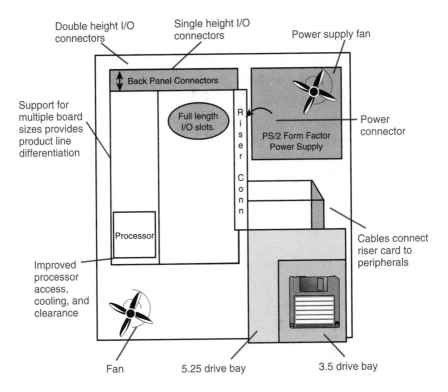

FIGURE 8.6   The basic layout of the NLX style motherboard.

INSTALLING YOUR NEW MOTHERBOARD

Regardless of which motherboard size or style you are purchasing to replace your existing motherboard, you need to plan the replacement carefully. Although replacing a motherboard may look like a major technological undertaking, in reality all you need is a little bit of planning and a bit more patience to get the job done. Remember to unplug your PC and ground yourself before you remove the PC's cover. Also make sure that you place all components removed from your motherboard someplace where they cannot be damaged physically or by static electricity.

To replace your existing motherboard, follow these steps:

1. The first task you need to perform is to make a diagram of all the connections (ribbon cables, jumpers, thin-wire cables, interface cards, and so on), paying particular attention to orientation of connectors—especially those connectors that can be attached more than one way, such as ribbon cables. Most ribbon cables have a red strip on one edge of the cable. This red strip is used to orient the first pin—called pin 1—to its correct position in the connector. Be sure to label or identify each connecting device attached to your motherboard.

2. Next read and re-read any and all instructions that come with your new motherboard. There may be steps you need to take either before or after you install the new motherboard.

3. Examine your existing motherboard in its case to see exactly how it is attached to the case. Notice number and position of screws and non-metallic connectors and supports.

4. Remove all interface cards from your motherboard by first removing the retaining screw and then gently lifting the card out of its slot. If any cables are attached to any interface cards, carefully remove and label the cables.

5. Carefully remove the memory and processor installed in your computer. If it is awkward to remove these now, you can wait until you have removed the motherboard from the case to remove the processor and memory.

6. One at a time remove any cables attached to your motherboard and label them.

Remember black One way to easily remember how to reattach the cables from your motherboard to the power supply is that the black wires are always on the inside next to each other.

7. When all components and connectors have been removed from your motherboard, remove the screws and standoff connectors holding your motherboard in its case. Carefully remove the motherboard from its case. Note the orientation of your motherboard to its case.

8. Place the new motherboard in your case, paying attention to any possible changes in the standoff connectors, and reverse the operations performed in steps 4–7.

   On some older motherboards users occasionally had problems with interface cards being placed over processors, but newer designs in motherboards rearranged placement of CPUs and cards to avoid this problem. The biggest problem you can encounter with replacing all your cards is making sure that the new motherboard has the same number of card slots as your old motherboard.

9. Perform any setup operations dictated by the instructions that were included with your new motherboard.

When you have reattached everything to your new motherboard that was removed from your old motherboard, you are now ready to turn on your PC and test your handy work. If your PC displays any error, note the error and check the instructions that came with your new motherboard. Recheck your work, and when you have corrected the problem causing the error, retest your PC.

In this lesson, you learned about motherboard replacement. You learned about the various types of motherboards and how to select one to replace your existing motherboard. In the next lesson, you learn about upgrading your hard disk drive.

9 LESSON

HARD DISK UPGRADES

In this lesson, you learn how to upgrade the hard disk drive in your PC.

IT'S TIME TO UPGRADE YOUR HARD DISK

There's never been a better time to upgrade your hard disk drive. Hard disk drive prices have been steadily dropping for years. In 1984, a Seagate 30MB hard disk could cost about $350. Now you can buy a hard disk drive 100 times larger for the same money or less.

Not only are newer hard disks cheaper, they are also faster—and programs seem to be getting larger as well.

If you have less than 3GB (gigabytes) of hard disk storage in your PC, then you definitely should consider buying a 2GB or 3GB drive—especially considering the price now of a new hard disk. If you have less than 1GB of disk storage space, then you are long overdue for a hard disk upgrade, and you owe yourself this minor indulgence.

 Gigabyte A gigabyte is a thousand megabytes and a megabyte is one million bytes, so a gigabyte is one billion bytes. Gigabyte is commonly abbreviated GB.

The same principle used in upgrading memory applies when upgrading your hard disk drive. In the majority of cases, you are actually adding a second hard disk rather than upgrading (replacing an older, smaller hard disk with a newer, larger hard disk).

The only reasons you should ever consider replacing your existing hard disk drive are:

- Your computer does not physically have room (an empty drive bay) for you to add a second hard disk drive.

- You are switching from an IDE hard disk drive to a SCSI hard disk drive.

IDE VERSUS SCSI

The first major decision you have to make in upgrading your hard disk is choosing between the two types—IDE and SCSI. The systems diagnostic/configuration program you ran in Lesson 3 should have identified the type of drive(s) you have in your PC.

 IDE and **SCSI**   IDE stands for Integrated Drive Electronics and SCSI stands for Small Computer System Interface. You might also see IDE listed as EIDE for Enhanced Integrated Drive Electronics, which is a newer and faster enhancement on the original IDE specification.

IDE is currently the more popular and widely used of the two disk types primarily because it is cheaper to manufacture. IDE also seems to have a slight edge in disk performance. Depending on how you have your PC configured and what operating system you plan to use, however, SCSI could actually give you better overall system performance. This is particularly true if you install two or more hard drives in your PC and you use a true 32-bit operating system, such as Windows NT 4.0 or 5.0.

IDE also offers another advantage for most PC users—virtually all desktop PCs shipping today ship with IDE disk controllers manufactured into the motherboard. Very few motherboards are manufactured with SCSI controllers built-in.

Disk controller   The interface that connects your disks to your motherboard. The controller can either be built into the motherboard or be in the form of a card installed into one of the slots on your motherboard.

Even though IDE drives are still slightly faster than SCSI drives, SCSI drives do have some pretty significant advantages over IDE drives:

- SCSI drives put far less strain on your CPU than do IDE drives, which can result in an overall higher level of system performance.

- SCSI drives perform better in 32-bit multitasking operating systems like Windows NT 4.0 and 5.0 because they can perform disk read and writing tasks while other operations and programs are running.

- You can attach up to seven SCSI drives or devices to a single controller; IDE drives and devices are limited to two per controller.

- A slower SCSI device, such as a CD-ROM drive, will not degrade the performance of a faster device (a hard disk, for example) if both are connected to the same controller. On IDE controllers, a CD-ROM will degrade the performance of a hard disk if both are on the same controller, which is why most PCs today are shipped with two IDE controllers on the motherboard.

- A SCSI cable can be up to 10 feet long, allowing you to install multiple external (outside of your PC) SCSI devices. IDE cable can usually be no longer than about 15 inches, which pretty well limits most IDE devices to being installed inside your PC.

Although SCSI drives can be configured to produce a higher level of performance, SCSI drives are still mainly used in network file servers rather than desktop PCs. Perhaps the biggest incentive for using IDE drives is cost. A comparable IDE drive can cost half the price of a SCSI drive. Also because SCSI controllers are rarely built in to motherboards, you will need to purchase a SCSI controller (minimum of about $100) in order to install SCSI drives.

INSTALLING AN IDE DRIVE

As mentioned earlier, you can install only two IDE drives or devices on a single IDE controller. Most manufacturers now build two IDE controllers on most motherboards (see Figure 9.1) so that you can install two hard disk drives on one controller and install a CD-ROM drive on the second controller.

FIGURE 9.1   Most motherboards now come equipped with two IDE controllers.

IDE drives use a series of jumpers on the drive to designate whether a single drive is installed on one controller or whether multiple drives are installed on the same controller. When multiple drives are installed on the same controller, one drive is designated the primary or "master," and the other drive is designated the secondary or "slave" (see Figure 9.2).

Figure 9.2 This figure shows jumpers on an IDE drive, which are used for specifying primary and secondary drives.

Replacing an Existing Drive

Replacing an existing drive with a newer drive is probably the easiest installation hardware-wise because the existing drive is the template you will follow for installing the new drive. In other words, notice how the drive you are removing is installed. Look and see how it is positioned in your case and see how the cables are attached to the drive. This is your model for installing the replacement drive.

When replacing an existing drive with a new drive, one of your first considerations should be to determine how you will transfer the files from the old drive to the new drive. If you have some sort of backup device (for example, a tape drive or removable media drive, such as a Zip drive), this will greatly simplify the file transfer process. If you do not have a backup device, then your only option is to back up your data files onto floppy disks and then re-install your operating system and programs onto the new drive after it is installed. There are a number of disk image copying programs on the market, such as Ghost, Partition Magic, and Drive Image, which can greatly simplify this task. These programs, however, usually require some sort of large storage or backup device to temporarily store the disk image. If you have access to a network file server, then these disk image copying programs can be a godsend.

Disk image program   Reads your hard disk drive and makes an exact copy of the drive contents sector by sector, regardless of what you have stored, and makes an exact copy of your drive byte for byte and notes where on your hard disk each byte is stored.

Regardless of which backup method you choose, just make sure you back up your files before you remove the existing hard disk drive.

To replace an existing drive, follow these steps:

1. Unplug your PC and ground yourself before removing the cover.

2. Remove the cover and locate the drive you are replacing.

3. Two cables should be attached to your existing hard disk—a four-wire power cable and a flat (usually gray) ribbon cable. Note how each cable is attached to your hard disk drive. The power cable can be attached only one way because of the design of the connector. The ribbon cable, however, can be attached two ways. To help you re-attach the ribbon cable correctly, notice that on one edge of the ribbon cable is a red stripe (see Figure 9.3). Note the position of the red stripe and make sure you attach the ribbon cable to the new drive in the same position as the ribbon cable is attached to the old drive.

Red stripe indicates the #1 pin position

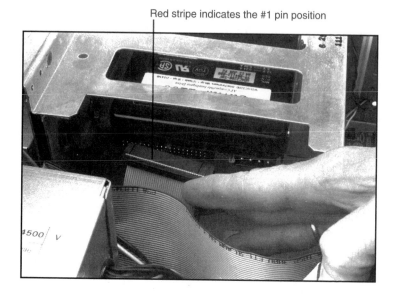

Figure 9.3   The hard disk ribbon cable often is marked with a red stripe to indicate the #1 pin position.

4. When you have diagrammed how the cables are attached to your existing drive, carefully remove the cables from the existing drive.

5. Notice how your existing hard disk drive is physically attached to the computer case. The hard disk might be enclosed in a support frame, it might be attached to a drawer-like apparatus, or it might simply have guide rails attached on either side. Locate the screws holding the hard disk drive in place or holding its support frame in place. Remove the screws and gently slide the drive out of its housing or support frame. Note how the drive is enclosed because you will need to enclose the new drive in the same manner.

6. Locate the jumper pins on the existing hard disk. If you are replacing a single drive, then the jumper pins should not have any jumpers installed. Make sure there are no jumpers installed on the jumper pins of the new drive.

If this drive shares an IDE connector with another IDE device, such as a CD-ROM drive, then a jumper will be installed on the jumper pins. If a jumper is installed, make sure that the new drive has the jumper in the same position. Again use the existing drive as your model and make sure that you place the jumper on the new drive in the same way that the jumper is installed on the existing drive.

7. After you have removed the old drive from its support frame (or removed the guide rails), install the new drive in place of the old drive.

8. Re-attach the drive support frame back into the case or slide the drive back into the position of the old drive.

9. Re-attach the power and ribbon cables to the new drive.

When you turn on your PC for the first time, you will probably have to re-run your CMOS hardware Setup program to configure the new drive. This procedure will vary from PC to PC—some newer PCs will do a considerable amount to automate this process whereas some older PCs may require you to enter hardware values for the new drive, such as the number of drive heads, tracks, and sectors. This information will be supplied with the drive, so make sure to hold onto your documentation.

That's it! You've not only just installed a new drive, but you've probably saved yourself $60-$100 in the process considering what you would have had to pay a computer technician to install the drive. All that's left now is to re-install your operating system, programs, and files. Just follow the instructions that came with your software to re-install it.

Adding a Second Drive

Adding a second drive is usually even easier than replacing an existing drive. Again you can use the existing drive as a template for how the new drive will be installed. When adding a second IDE drive, remember that one drive has to be designated the primary or master and the other drive has to be designated the

secondary or slave. In most cases, the existing drive will be designated the master and the drive you are adding will be designated
the slave. By designating the new drive as the secondary or slave,
you do not need to concern yourself with backing up the files on
the existing drive or installing an operating system on the new
drive. The new drive (after it is formatted) will simply appear as
the next drive letter after your existing drive (usually drive D:).

Which drive letter? If you have a CD-ROM drive and
you are adding a new hard disk drive, your CD-ROM drive
will be bumped to the next letter. For example, If your CD-
ROM drive is D:, after you add another hard disk drive,
the hard disk will become D: and your CD-ROM drive will
become E:. Usually this is not a problem except for software you install from a CD-ROM, which requires you to
leave the CD-ROM in the drive while the program is running (like many games). In this scenario your program will
be looking for your CD-ROM files on drive D: instead of
drive E:. If this happens to you, see if there is a way to
reconfigure your program to look on E: from the CD-ROM.
If you can't reconfigure, then you will have to re-install.

You will also need to note how the ribbon cable is attached to the
existing drive and attach the ribbon cable in the same position to
the new drive you are adding. Note, too, that two connectors are
on the ribbon cable for attaching IDE devices. Because you are
designating one drive the master and one drive the slave, it does
not matter which connector you attach the new drive to (see Figure 9.4).

Just make sure before you begin that your PC has sufficient physical room for a second drive and make sure you have all of the
mounting hardware (for example, support frame, guide rails, and
so on) before you begin. Many hard disk drive kits now come
with several sets of mounting hardware to cover all contingencies,
but it never hurts to tell the sales rep what type of computer you
have to ensure that the kit you purchase will work with your system. Most computer stores that sell hard disk drives also sell

mounting kits, and the kits usually identify most of the computers they are designed to work with.

Also, if you find yourself missing a 4-wire power cable, you can pick up a Y-connector (see Figure 9.5) at most any computer store for around $5.

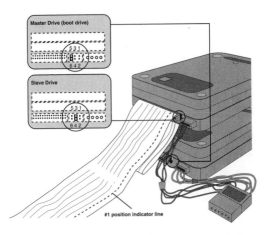

FIGURE 9.4   This figure shows two IDE drives and the positioning of jumpers and ribbon cable.

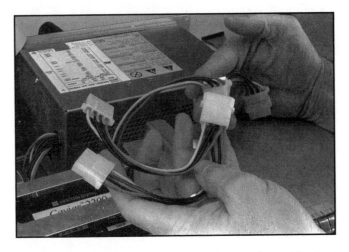

FIGURE 9.5   A simple Y-connector can be purchased for just a few dollars.

INSTALLING A SCSI DRIVE

When you install SCSI devices in your PC, you are creating what is called a "SCSI chain." The chain consists of a SCSI controller card, a SCSI cable, one or more SCSI devices, and a SCSI terminator at each end of the chain. It is important to remember that the terminators are always at both ends of the SCSI chain. I mention this because the end of a SCSI chain can be

- A SCSI controller card

- A SCSI device such as a hard disk drive, a CD-ROM drive, a tape backup drive, a scanner, and so on

- A SCSI terminator

Most newer SCSI controller cards are designed with both an internal and external connector for attaching SCSI devices (see Figure 9.6). Because of this design, a SCSI controller card can be in the middle of your SCSI chain or at either end, depending on whether you have internal or external SCSI devices or both. Most newer SCSI controller cards can also be self-terminating if they are at the end of the SCSI chain.

 Terminator   An electronic component that signals the end (both ends) of the SCSI chain.

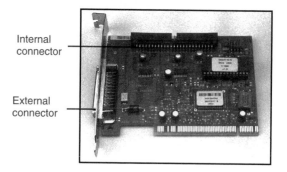

Internal connector

External connector

FIGURE 9.6   A SCSI controller card with both an internal and external connector.

Every device on a SCSI chain has to have a unique ID number. SCSI ID numbers are simply of means of identifying one device from another. For example, if you have two cats, you would not name them both Max because they would get confused when you called them. The same applies to SCSI devices. Unless they have unique ID numbers, confusion could occur when one drive needed to be accessed.

In most cases the SCSI controller is given the SCSI ID number 7, which means you can use ID numbers 0–6 for your SCSI devices. For hard disk drives, SCSI ID numbers usually are set using a series of jumpers. The instructions accompanying the drive will explain how to install the jumpers for a specific ID number. You do not designate a SCSI drive as master or slave as you do with IDE drives. If you plan to boot your PC from the SCSI drive, its ID number usually must be set to 0. If you have both IDE and SCSI drives in your PC, you must boot your PC from the IDE drive, in which case the SCSI drive ID can be any number from 0–6.

Physically installing the SCSI drive into your PC is about the same as installing an IDE in regards to physical location and mounting hardware. You may have a bit more latitude here because SCSI cables can be a lot longer than IDE cables.

To install an internal SCSI hard disk, follow these steps:

1. Install the SCSI controller card in an empty slot.

2. Set the SCSI ID on the drive according to how you plan to use it (will you boot from the SCSI drive, will the SCSI drive exist in the PC with an IDE drive, and so on). In most cases the ID number is set using jumpers.

3. Install the SCSI drive using the mounting hardware you have.

4. Attach the power cable to the SCSI drive.

5. Attach the SCSI cable to the drive. In every case I have ever seen, SCSI cables are notched or in some way designed so that the cable can be attached only one way.

6. If the internal SCSI drive is the only SCSI device you are installing, make sure that the SCSI cable (SCSI chain) is terminated after the drive. Make sure the other end of the SCSI chain, which should be the SCSI controller, is also terminated. Many newer SCSI controllers will self-terminate if they are at the end of the SCSI chain.

 If you install an external SCSI device, such as a scanner, then termination would no longer be at the controller card but at (or after) the last external device. Likewise, if you install an additional internal SCSI device such as a SCSI CD-ROM drive after the hard disk on the SCSI chain, then the termination would now fall after the last device on the chain. Just remember, terminate **both** ends of the SCSI chain.

If the SCSI drive is the only drive in your PC, you will not have to make any changes in your CMOS settings unless you are removing an IDE drive and replacing it with a SCSI drive. In that case, you will have to turn off or disable all IDE parameters (settings). You would need to run your hardware Setup (CMOS) program and in most cases set your IDE drive settings to "unused" or "disabled."

 IDE parameters The setting you make in your hardware Setup (CMOS) program to identify the characteristics of your drive. These include the number of read-write heads on your drive, the number of physical platters (the metal disks which actually make up your hard disk), and the number of tracks and sectors defined on each platter surface. The surface of each hard disk platter is divided into a number of concentric rings. These rings are tracks. Each track in turn is again divided into a number of wedge-shaped units called sectors.

PREPARING THE DRIVE FOR SOFTWARE

Before you can install files and software onto your new drive, you need to create one or more disk partitions, using FDISK or a similar utility, and format the drive. A partition is nothing more than a defined area on your hard disk that you will use to store files. If you use FDISK (which is stored on your DOS disk), you simply boot your computer using your DOS disk and then start FDISK by typing FDISK at the DOS prompt. Select the option to create a partition, which in most cases you would create a single partition and use your entire hard disk. Follow the instructions accompanying the operating system you plan to use on how to prepare your hard disk.

In this lesson, you learned how to install a new hard drive in your PC, either as a replacement drive or as a second drive. You also learned the differences between IDE and SCSI hard disks and how to decide which drive type to put in your computer. In the next lesson, you learn how to replace a floppy disk drive in your PC.

10

REPLACING A FLOPPY DISK DRIVE

In this lesson, you learn how to replace a floppy disk drive in your PC.

REPLACING NOT UPGRADING

The previous lessons have mainly been concerned with upgrading components in your PC, such as removing an older component and replacing it with a newer, more technologically advanced component. In this lesson you'll be dealing solely with replacing a floppy disk drive with another, identical floppy disk drive.

Since the original IBM PC was replaced back in 1981, floppy disk drives have evolved considerably. The first PCs were equipped with single-sided drives with a capacity of only 160K. In the next few years floppy disk drives on PCs evolved as you see in Table 10.1.

TABLE 10.1

TYPE	CAPACITY	SIZE
Single-sided, single density, 8 tracks	160KB	5 1/4"
Single-sided, single density, 9 tracks	180KB	5 1/4"
Double-sided, single density, 8 tracks	320KB	5 1/4"
Double-sided, single density, 9 tracks	360KB	5 1/4"
Double-sided, double density	720KB	3 1/2"
Double-sided, double density	1.2MB	3 1/2"
Double-sided, double density	1.44MB	3 1/2"

There have been a few advancements since the original 1.44M, 3 1/2-inch drive was released, but the industry seems to have settled on this model as its standard. And if you've used a computer for more than a few years, you may have also noticed how the industry phased out the 5 1/4-inch drive.

In the past few years, many books on upgrading PCs have included chapters on repairing floppy disk drives. But now that floppy disk drives have been reduced to commodity status and can be readily purchased at most weekend computer fairs for as little as $10, it makes little sense to worry about repairing what has literally become a "throw-away" computer component.

 Always keep a spare Even though floppy disk drives are not as essential to day-to-day computer operations as they once were, at roughly $10 a pop it makes good sense to keep a spare on hand as an emergency repair unit. Remember that when you upgrade your PC, you should keep your floppy as a spare.

REPLACING A BROKEN FLOPPY DISK DRIVE

Replacing a broken floppy disk drive is as simple, if not simpler, than installing a hard disk drive (see Lesson 9). To replace a floppy disk drive, follow these steps:

1. Unplug your PC and ground yourself before removing the cover.

2. Examine your PC to see how the floppy disk drive is installed in your computer's case. Note how many screws are holding the drive in place and the cables attached to the drive.

3. Identify (and label if necessary) where and how the cables are attached to the drive before you carefully remove the cables. If you have to remove any other cables to gain

access to your floppy disk drive, make note of these also. Notice that the power connector for a 3 1/2-inch drive is smaller than the standard power connector (see Figure 10.1).

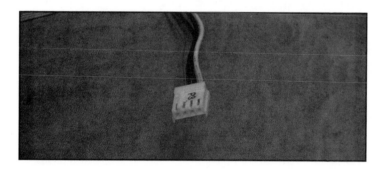

Figure 10.1 Shown here is a power connector for a 3 1/2" floppy disk drive.

4. Remove all screws holding the drive in place (see Figure 10.2) and carefully remove the drive from the computer case.

Figure 10.2 Remove the mounting screws.

5. Insert the new drive and replace and reconnect everything you removed and disconnected in steps 1–4.

When everything has been re-attached and reconnected, turn on your PC to test your work. Notice if the light on the drive comes on when you restart your PC. If the light comes on and stays on, it means you have the ribbon cable on backwards. If this happens, simply turn off and unplug your computer, open the case, and reverse the ribbon cable. When you re-assemble the power up, everything should work fine. Place a floppy disk into the new drive and perform a few routine tests on the drive. Try issuing the DIR A: command from the DOS prompt to see if the computer reads the contents of the disk. If you are using Windows 95 or NT, you can use Explorer to test your drive. Try formatting a disk in the drive and then try copying a few files to the disk. If all of these tests work satisfactorily, then you can be fairly certain that the disk you just installed is working OK.

In this lesson, you learned how to replace a floppy disk drive in your PC. In the next lesson, you learn how to select and install a CD-ROM drive in your PC.

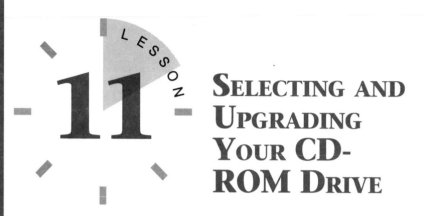

SELECTING AND UPGRADING YOUR CD-ROM DRIVE

In this lesson, you learn how to select and replace a CD-ROM drive in your PC.

SELECTING A GOOD CD-ROM DRIVE

Despite all of the hoopla you've read and heard about *DVD* drives replacing CD-ROM drives and making them obsolete, it hasn't happened yet. Considering the rate at which manufacturers are still cranking out CD-ROM drives, this switch to DVD technology isn't going to happen overnight.

 DVD *Digital Video Disk* is a rather new digital technology very similar to CD-ROM technology. DVDs differ in that they are able to store several times the capacity of CD-ROM disks—approximately 650MB.

Not too long ago a CD-ROM drive was considered a multimedia luxury; but with more and more manufacturers now distributing software on CDs, a CD-ROM drive is a necessity. You may have also noticed that most new computer systems now include a CD-ROM drive as standard equipment.

DETERMINING A CD-ROM DRIVE'S SPEED

CD-ROM drives are not just available, they are plentiful. One reason they are so plentiful is that manufacturers keep "upping the ante" by continually trying to produce faster and faster drives.

It is hard to quote a number as being the "standard" speed of CD-ROM drives, but many CD-ROM drives being sold now are stated to have a *transfer speed* of between 20x and 24x.

 Transfer speed   The number usually quoted on how fast a CD-ROM drive is, such as 12x, 16x, 20x, 24x. The transfer speed is how fast the drive can move data from the CD to the CPU, measured in kilobytes per second in units of 150K/s. For example, 1x equals 150K/s, and 12x equals 12 times 150K/s, or 1800K/s.

Even though transfer speeds of between 20x and 24x are advertised, not all drives live up to their advertising. In general it is best to purchase the fastest drive you can afford. If you want an honest appraisal of how various models of CD-ROM drives perform, check out the multitude of product reviews frequently published in most of the popular PC magazines.

Transfer speed is not the only factor you should use in your selection of a CD-ROM drive because transfer speed is not the only factor that affects a CD-ROM drive's performance. The other factors you should consider, in order of their importance, are:

- *Average seek time or access time.* The time in milliseconds between when a request is made for data on the CD and when the data is found and delivered. A good access time is 110ms; anything lower is excellent.

- *Buffer or cache.* A holding area of memory built into the drive to temporarily store data as it is being processed. Most drives have a cache of about 256K; anything larger is a premium.

SCSI VERSUS IDE

Just as you had to decide between IDE and SCSI when you were selecting a hard disk drive in Lesson 9, when selecting a CD-ROM drive you also have to decide between IDE and SCSI. The same factors concerning performance and cost you had to consider when selecting a hard disk interface apply just as much when selecting a CD-ROM type (see Lesson 9).

If you already have a SCSI controller in your PC, you will be way ahead in terms of performance with a SCSI CD-ROM drive.

INSTALLING THE DRIVE IN YOUR PC—INTERNAL VERSUS EXTERNAL

If you plan to install a CD-ROM drive with an IDE interface, then the decision on internal versus external has already been made for you. All IDE CD-ROM drives are internal because the IDE interface does not allow for a cable long enough to connect an external drive. Another major advantage an internal drive has over an external drive is cost. An internal drive is generally $75–$100 cheaper than an external drive because an external CD-ROM drive requires a case and separate power supply. The only real consideration you have for installing an internal drive is whether your PC has physical room for an internal drive. Internal CD-ROM drives are all a standard size and will occupy what is called a full-sized drive bay slot (see Figure 11.1).

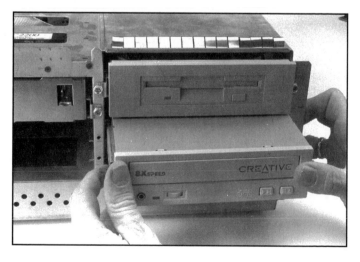

FIGURE 11.1   An internal CD-ROM drive in a drive bay slot.

Installing an internal CD-ROM drive is no more difficult than installing a hard disk drive. To install an internal drive, follow these steps:

1. Select a drive bay in your PC that you can use to install the drive. Make sure that you remove the front panel on the case covering the empty bay if there is one. Make sure you also have an unused power connector you can plug into the drive. If you don't have an unused power connector, go to a local computer store and pick up a Y-connector. Unplug one of your power connectors from another device and attach the Y-connector.

2. On most PCs built in the last three or four years, you will find two IDE interfaces usually labeled primary and secondary (see Figure 11.2). Your hard disk drive (if you have an IDE hard disk installed in your PC) should be attached via cable to the interface labeled primary. Make sure you have a cable that will reach from the secondary interface to the bay where you are installing your drive.

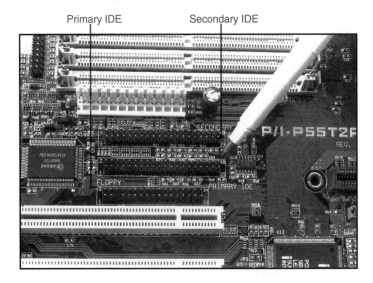

Figure 11.2   Primary and secondary IDE interfaces on motherboard.

3. If you have to install any guide rails on the sides of your drive, install them according to the instructions accompanying the drive (see Figure 11.3). If drive rails are not included, be sure to pick up a set from your local computer store.

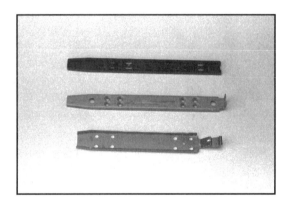

FIGURE 11.3   Various sized guide rails used to secure drives.

4. Insert the drive into the drive bay and attach the ribbon cable from the secondary (slave) IDE interface to the 40-pin IDE interface on the rear of the drive (see Figure 11.4). Connect the power connector.

Sound card connection   40-pin IDE interface   4-pin power connection

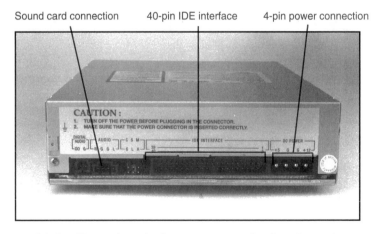

FIGURE 11.4   Shown here is the rear connection interface of a typical IDE CD-ROM drive.

Only one IDE interface? Don't panic if you find that you only have a single IDE interface on your motherboard. A single interface can accommodate two IDE devices, but if you are connecting both a hard disk drive and a CD-ROM drive, the lower CD-ROM drive will degrade performance of your hard disk. The solution is to purchase an IDE interface card at your local computer store for around $25.

5. If you also have a sound card in your PC (see Lesson 19), you can also connect the audio cable to the audio connector on the rear of the CD-ROM drive. Without the audio cable, you will not be able to play audio on CDs through your sound system.

6. After you have everything connected to your drive, adjust your drive even with the front opening of the drive bay and tighten the screws holding your drive in place.

Just as you did when you installed your hard disk drive, you will probably have to run your computer's hardware Setup program. Also, you should have some type of software installation disk, which you will need to run to install the appropriate driver depending on the operating system you are running.

 Windows 95 may install driver automatically If you are running Windows 95 on your PC, it is very likely that when you start Windows 95 it will detect the presence of a new CD-ROM drive and automatically install the appropriate driver for you (a feature known as Plug and Play). Just make sure that you have your original Windows 95 installation disks on hand.

Play music CDs   In addition to a hardware driver for your drive, the disk that comes with your CD-ROM drive also includes a number of utilities for your drive. One of the most enjoyable utilities is one that allows you to also play music CDs on your new drive. If you don't have a sound card in your PC, you can simply plug a set of headphones into the connector on the front of the drive next to the volume control, provided your CD-ROM drive has one.

INSTALLING AN INTERNAL SCSI DRIVE

Installing an internal SCSI CD-ROM drive is almost exactly the same as installing an internal IDE drive except that the cable is different and you have to set the SCSI ID on the drive according to the instructions that came with your drive.

Check your SCSI ID   All SCSI devices leave the factory with a pre-set SCSI ID, which in most cases you can leave as is. But it never hurts to make sure that the ID set on the drive isn't an ID you are already using on your SCSI chain.

Remember that just like with a SCSI hard disk drive, the SCSI chain (see Lesson 9) you attach your CD-ROM drive to has to be terminated at both ends.

INSTALLING AN EXTERNAL DRIVE (SCSI ONLY)

Installing an external drive is even easier than installing an internal drive. External drives are always SCSI drives and almost always ship with the appropriate cable you will need to connect your drive.

Need a SCSI interface card? Many external SCSI CD-ROM drives also ship with a SCSI interface card, which saves you the trouble and expense of having to purchase one separately. If you find that you do have to purchase a SCSI interface card, check with the manufacturer of the drive to see if any types of SCSI cards are recommended.

After you have the drive, cable, and interface card, literally all you have to do is insert the card into an empty slot in your PC, and then connect one end of the cable to the connector on the end of the card (the connector protruding out of the back of your PC) and the other end of the cable to the connector on the drive. With some SCSI CD-ROM drives, you will receive a SCSI terminator. The terminator looks like the plug on the end of the SCSI cable without the cable attached. If you need to use the terminator to terminate your SCSI chain, you will see two SCSI connectors on the back of the SCSI CD-ROM drive. Plug the terminator into one connector and plug the SCSI cable into the other connector.

Check end of SCSI chain Only the device at the end of the SCSI chain is terminated. If the CD-ROM drive is not at the end of the SCSI chain, you will not have to terminate the chain at the drive.

Now just plug in the electrical cord, run the Setup program for your PC, and then install the driver for the CD-ROM drive from the disk included with your drive and you're done.

Windows 95 Plug and Play If you are using Windows 95 and if your CD-ROM drive and SCSI card are Plug and Play, Windows 95 should recognize the additional hardware when you restart your PC. Follow the prompts on-screen to install the CD-ROM drive.

In this lesson, you learned about some of the choices you need to consider when selecting a CD-ROM drive and how to install both an internal and an external drive. In the next lesson, you learn about removable media drives.

Adding a Removable Drive

*In this lesson, you learn about
removable media and how to add a removable drive to your PC.*

What are Removable Media Drives?

Just a few years ago, if you mentioned removable media you were undoubtedly talking about either floppy disks or tape backup. Removable media then were either small in capacity or limited in functionality. Well, times have changed. Now you can get removable media that resemble hard disk drives both in capacity and in functionality. Of course, you can also still get removable media in the form of floppy disks and tape backup devices.

The focus of this lesson is on tape backup drives and the assortment of high-capacity removable hard disk-like drives (Zip drives, for example).

Tape Backup Drives

Tape backup drives today come in an assortment of sizes and capacities. At one time tape backup drives were almost exclusively used to back up network file servers, but are growing in popularity among individual computer users now that hard disk drives have grown in size to where it is inconceivable to think of backing them up using floppy disks.

Choosing a tape backup drive is still largely a matter of what you want to pay for. An expensive tape backup drive won't back up any better than a cheaper model, but an expensive drive will most likely back up your hard disk faster and possibly use fewer tapes.

Tape drives come as both internal and external models, and use both IDE and SCSI interfaces. A few tape drives come with their own proprietary interface. There are even external tape drives that plug into the parallel port on the back of your computer.

EXTERNAL TAPE DRIVES

The parallel port type drives are probably the easiest type of tape drive to install because all you do is plug the drive into the parallel port and then install the tape backup software. You don't have to worry about connecting cables, running your PC's Setup program, or even taking the cover off your PC. The drawback to these types of tape drives is speed—they are among the slowest tape drives on the market. But most users get around this limitation by performing their backups overnight.

Most other external tape drives use a SCSI interface and install pretty much the same way as an external CD-ROM drive (see Lesson 11). All you need to do is set the tape drive to use an available SCSI ID number and plug it into your SCSI card.

INTERNAL TAPE DRIVES

Internal tape drives use IDE, SCSI, and proprietary interfaces. Internal drives are installed pretty much the same as internal CD-ROM drives. You must take into account the same considerations, such as an available drive bay, reach of the interface cable, and so on (see Figure 12.1).

SCSI tape drives are typically faster and more expensive than IDE drives, so take this into consideration when deciding what type to purchase. Remember that with a SCSI drive you will need a SCSI interface card if you don't already have one (see Figure 12.2).

The tape drive's data cable   The tape drive's power cable

FIGURE 12.1   An internal tape drive is being inserted into a drive bay.

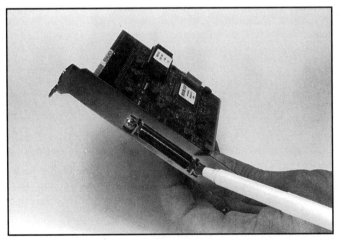

FIGURE 12.2   A SCSI interface card.

When deciding on what type of tape drive to get, pay attention to the capacity of the tapes each drive uses (see Figure 12.3). Although the general rule of thumb is that you should be able to back up each hard disk drive in your PC with one tape, all tape backup software will allow you to span a backup session across multiple tapes. It's just easier and more convenient to use one tape, especially if you perform your backups overnight.

FIGURE 12.3   A typical tape cartridge.

REMOVABLE HARD DISK DRIVES

Removable hard disk drives have become extremely popular in the last year or two mainly because the price of these drives has dropped and because some models come extremely close to duplicating the performance of standard hard disk drives. The popularity of removable hard disk drives has also begun to erode the tape drive market. The most popular removable hard disk drives are made by Iomega and SyQuest. Both companies produce low-end and high-end models. Iomega produces the most popular low-end model—the Zip drive.

Zip drive cartridges are capable of storing 100MB of data, and the drives are available in both internal and external models. The external models use either a SCSI or parallel port interface.

The internal models use either a SCSI or IDE interface. Zip drives are typically installed as a backup device because their performance is not quite up to par with standard hard disk drives—especially the models using an IDE or parallel port interface, which are somewhat slower than the SCSI models.

You install the SCSI models using the same procedures as you would in installing a SCSI CD-ROM drive (see Lesson 11). The IDE model Zip drive installs the same as an IDE model CD-ROM drive. To install a Zip drive with a parallel port interface, you merely plug the drive into your parallel port and install the software.

Iomega also manufactures the most popular high-end model removable hard disk drive—the Jaz drive (see Figure 12.4). The Zip and the Jaz drives are similar in appearance, but typically have different color cases.

FIGURE 12.4   An external Jaz drive.

The original Jaz drive used a cartridge capable of storing 1GB of data, and its performance closely rivaled that of standard hard disk drives. To achieve this kind of performance, the Jaz drive is only available with a SCSI interface. In late 1997, Iomega released a new model of its Jaz drive to counter competition from SyQuest. The SyQuest model, the SyJet, equals the performance of the Jaz drive and uses a cartridge capable of storing 1.5GB of data. Iomega's new model, the Jaz-2, also utilizes a SCSI interface and uses a cartridge capable of storing 2GB of data.

Because both the Jaz models and the SyJet equal the performance of many hard disk drives, it is possible to use them in place of standard hard disk drives. You install them the same as you would any other SCSI device (see Lessons 9 and 11). You can also install Jaz or SyJet drives as your primary hard disk drive. To boot any of these drives, though, you need to set the SCSI ID number to 0; and like booting to a standard SCSI hard disk drive, you cannot combine SCSI and IDE hard disk drives in the same PC.

In this lesson, you learned about removable media drives—tape backup drives and removable hard disk drives. In the next lesson, you learn about selecting a new pointing device for your PC.

REPLACING YOUR INPUT DEVICES

*In this lesson, you learn about
replacing your computer's main input devices, keyboard, and mouse.*

WHAT'S WRONG WITH THE KEYBOARD AND MOUSE THAT CAME WITH MY PC?

You might think that this may be one lesson you want to skip because there's nothing wrong with the keyboard and mouse that came with your PC. Well the idea is not that there's anything wrong with your keyboard and mouse, but there are replacement keyboards and mice that can make using your PC for long hours easier and a much more pleasant experience.

Keyboards and mice have improved considerably over the past few years, both in functionality and *ergonomics*.

 Ergonomics The study of the relationship between people and their work environments. In simpler terms, it has come to mean producing tools used in the workplace, such as chairs, desks, and keyboards, that conform more to the way human bodies are designed rather than making human bodies conform to workplace tools. The idea is to increase comfort and reduce injuries and stress.

KEYBOARDS

Perhaps the most radical change that has occurred in keyboards is the introduction of the so-called natural, or ergonomic, keyboards (see Figure 13.1).

FIGURE 13.1   A natural ergonomic keyboard.

There are a number of companies now producing ergonomic keyboards. The basic idea behind the keyboard is that it places your hands into a more natural position of having your palms face each other, which places much less stress on the ligaments in your wrists and hands. Another direction many manufacturers are going with keyboard design is added functionality. Keyboards are no longer "just keyboards." You can now purchase keyboards with additional devices built-in, such as scanners (see Figure 13.2) and audio speakers.

Whether you purchase a keyboard for more comfort and functionality, or if you are just looking for a keyboard with a better "feel" than the one you currently are using, you need to make sure that you get a keyboard with the correct type of plug for your PC. Most PCs today are manufactured with ports for the newer, smaller 6-pin PS/2 style keyboard plugs (see Figure 13.3).

FIGURE 13.2   A keyboard with integrated sheetfed scanner. *(Photo courtesy of NMB Technologies.)*

FIGURE 13.3   Shown here is the 6-pin PS/2 style keyboard plug.

The other type of keyboard plug is the original AT style plug, which is noticeably larger than the PS/2 plug (see Figure 13.4).

FIGURE 13.4   Shown here is the larger, AT-style keyboard plug.

Wrong plug?   Don't panic if you purchase a new keyboard and when you attempt to plug it, your new keyboard has the wrong plug. Most computer stores sell keyboard plug adapters for $5-10 that will convert PS/2 to AT and vice versa.

MICE AND OTHER POINTING DEVICES

For many users, their mouse is purely a functional device—either it is functioning or it isn't. However, mice today offer a lot more than mere functionality. There are ergonomic mice designed to fit your hand. There are cordless mice so you don't have to worry about the cord getting in your way. There are mice with two buttons. There are mice with three buttons. There are mice for left-handed users. There are even mice with built-in gyroscopic mechanisms you can wave through the air instead of dragging across a pad.

One of the newer mouse innovations for people who frequently surf the World Wide Web is a mouse with a special scrolling wheel placed between the two buttons. The scrolling wheel allows you to scroll up and down long Web pages quickly and smoothly.

 It acts like a scrolling wheel   If you are using Windows 95 or Windows NT 4.0, you can run a program that allows most mice to behave as if they have a scrolling wheel. Go to **http://www.pontix.com** and download the Pointix Scroll 1.0 utility.

If you prefer to move your hand rather than move your pointing device, you can also opt to install a *trackball* rather than a mouse (see Figure 13.5).

 Trackball   Simply stated, this is a mouse upside down. The ball inside the pointing device is not moved across a pad, but instead the ball is moved by your hand motions.

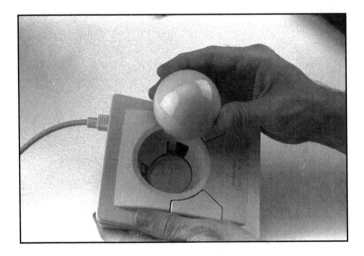

FIGURE 13.5   This picture shows a typical trackball.

Getting a new mouse to fit your PC is much easier than getting a new keyboard to fit. Mice also can fit into one of two types of connectors on your PC—what's called a 6-pin Din connector and a 9-pin serial connector. To give you the option of using either type connector, most manufacturers now include an adapter with their mice (see Figure 13.6).

FIGURE 13.6   A mouse port adapter.

What's most important when selecting a new mouse is comfort. Many large computer stores have a wide selection of mice on display that you can handle to see how they feel. Take this opportunity to try different sizes and styles of mice.

In this lesson, you learned abut selecting a new keyboard and a new mouse. In the next lesson, you learn about upgrading your video card.

Upgrading Your Video Card

In this lesson, you learn about selecting a new video card for your PC.

What's Currently Available in Video Cards

Today it is extremely difficult to purchase a bad video card. Video cards have been one of the fastest developing technologies in the computer industry in recent years, and this advancement surprisingly has been driven by the computer gaming industry.

Video cards Also referred to as video adapters, graphic adapters, and graphic cards. These terms all refer to the same device, the interface card in your computer that controls and produces video on your monitor.

Computer games and the demand they bring for faster and more complex graphics and animation have been pushing the video development envelope for the past few years. Consequently, the entire computer industry has benefited from the demands of this small segment of the industry because these same video cards also deliver improved graphic performance for the more mainstream business uses of computers.

The buzzword now in video cards is *3D graphics*, which refers to a means of displaying onscreen graphic objects so that they appear to have texture and appear more realistic. Again, the gaming side of the computer industry appears years ahead of the business side in terms of its use of 3D graphics.

WHAT TO LOOK FOR IN A VIDEO CARD

You currently need to look for two main features in selecting a video card—memory and speed. It's fairly easy to determine how much memory each video card has installed. The amount of memory installed on the card is usually printed in big, bold letters on the outside of the box. Many, if not most, video cards leave the factory with either 2MB or 4MB of memory installed. Video memory is also usually referred to as VRAM.

 VRAM Short for Video RAM (Random Access Memory), this is a special type of high-speed memory designed for use in video cards.

Memory is important because it directly controls video resolution and the number of colors displayed on your monitor. Resolution is defined as the number of pixels (short for picture elements) displayed onscreen. A pixel is the smallest unit that can be displayed onscreen. In standard VGA mode, 640 pixels are displayed horizontally by 480 pixels displayed vertically onscreen for a total of 307,200 pixels (640×480=307,000). When you increase resolution to 800×600, the number of pixels increases to 480,000. But the number of pixels displayed onscreen is only half the story. Each pixel is made up of a color. In 16-color mode, the lowest number of colors for VGA, each pixel can be 1 of 16 possible colors. You need 4 bits of memory to support 16-color mode, and if you do the math you will see that you need 153,600 bytes of memory to support 16-color mode (640×480=307,000×4=1,228,800(bits)/8=153,600(bytes)).

Unfortunately, 16-color mode does not produce very brilliant colors. A better color mode is 256 colors. To produce 256-color mode, however, you need 8 bits per pixel or 307,200 bytes of memory. Your display is getting better but still not great. An improvement would be to increase your color depth to 65,536 colors, but to do this you need 16 bits of memory for each pixel for a total of 614,400 bytes of memory. No one manufactures video cards with 614,400 bytes of memory. Instead, they round this number up to a more convenient 1MB of memory. So to display VGA resolution at 65,536 (64K) colors, you need 1MB of memory on your video card. If you increase your resolution to 1,024×768 at 64K colors, you now need 2MB of memory on your video card. If you increase your resolution to 1,280×1,024, then you need 4MB of memory on your video card.

Speed is important for a video card because a faster card will be able to redraw or refresh your display screen and produce smoother animation when you are displaying moving objects onscreen. Again, this is a feature more important to graphic artist programs, web graphics applications, CAD engineering software, and video games than to a word processing program. But video speed is also important if you are working in any type of business graphic program or if you are viewing graphics or animation on the Internet. The bottom line is that any application will benefit from a higher quality video card (especially Windows), and sooner or later you will be faced with using some sort of graphical application.

Video card speed is a little harder to determine. Often it takes sophisticated testing programs to determine the relative speed of a particular video card. Most users lack the testing software and resources to test numerous video cards, so you must rely on the various computer industry journals to test and publish their results. These testing reviews can often be valuable sources of information that you as a consumer and computer user should regularly check before making any computer purchase.

 Check the trade magazines   A few magazines you might care to browse for product reviews are *PC Magazine*, *PC World*, *Windows Magazine*, *Windows Sources*, and *Windows NT Magazine*.

WHY YOU WOULD WANT TO UPGRADE YOUR VIDEO CARD

So, what does all this mean in terms of trying to decide whether you need a new video card? If you are an ardent gamer and you are trying to keep pace with the latest gaming technology, then you will likely want the fastest video card you can get with at least 4MB of memory and that can display 3D graphics. If you are using any type of sophisticated graphics or animation software, then you will also want to consider upgrading to a video card that fits the same bill. An even less demanding reason technologically for upgrading your video card is purchasing a larger monitor. Although VGA is acceptable on a 14- or 15-inch monitor, if you are looking at a 17-, 19-, or even a 21-inch monitor, you will want to increase the resolution to a higher level in order to take advantage of your larger display. For monitors 17 inches and larger, it is fairly common to use a resolution of 1,024×768 or higher. If you look back at the last section, you will see that higher resolution and higher color depth require a video card with more memory. You can refer to Lesson 3 and the use of PC Doctor to determine the specifics of your existing video card.

INSTALLING A VIDEO CARD

Very little setup is involved in installing a new video card. Just follow these steps:

1. Turn off and unplug your PC. Ground yourself and then remove the cover.

2. Unplug the cable from your monitor, which is connected to your current video card.

3. Remove your current video card and insert the new video card into the same slot on your motherboard, as shown in Figure 14.1.

Disable built-in video cards   Some motherboards have built-in video cards, which you will need to disable before adding an upgraded video card. To disable a built-in video card, you need to consult the documentation that came with your PC. In many instances, you can disable a built-in video card by running the hardware Setup program used to configure your PC. To disable some built-in video cards, however, the manufacturer might have included a special video configuration utility.

FIGURE 14.1   Insert the new video card into the same slot on your computer's motherboard.

4.   Re-attach the video cable to your monitor and replace the cover on your PC.

Your new video card should include a disk containing the appropriate driver for the operating system you are using. Follow the instructions for installing the new video driver.

In this lesson, you learned how to upgrade your video card. But this is only half of the equation in upgrading your video system. A new video card (providing that it is an upgraded card) will allow you to see your graphics and games as you've never seen them before. But to truly appreciate your new video card, you will likely also need or at least want to upgrade your monitor as well. In the next lesson, you learn about selecting a new large-screen monitor to complement that new video card.

Getting a Larger Monitor

In this lesson, you learn about selecting a larger monitor for your PC.

Why You Should Purchase a Larger Monitor

In the last lesson, you learned about upgrading your video card. You also learned that to fully appreciate many video card upgrades, you should consider upgrading to larger monitor (larger than a 14- or 15-inch monitor). The basic reason you want to get a new, larger monitor is that a new, larger monitor will permit you to see more of your work.

For example, if you are currently using a 15-inch monitor, upgrading to a 17-inch monitor may not seem like much of an upgrade, but a 17-inch monitor will give you about 30 percent more onscreen viewing area. Upgrading from a 15-inch to a 21-inch monitor will give you more than 50 percent more onscreen viewing area.

Larger monitors also have been dropping in price in the past year. A good 17-inch monitor can be purchased now in the range of $500–$800. A good 21-inch monitor can be purchased now for $1,200–$1,800.

How big is too big? There is a downside to purchasing a larger monitor (besides the cost). A larger monitor takes up more room on your desktop and larger monitors, some 21-inch models, can weigh up to 75–80 lb.

SELECTING A NEW MONITOR

You need to know a few things before you go out and plop down your hard-earned cash for a new monitor.

A short time ago, the big buzzword for monitors was *dot pitch*. A computer monitor's screen is composed of thousands of very small dots, which when set to the correct color create the appearance of images. Dot pitch is the measurement between these dots. Unfortunately, not every manufacturer measures dot pitch the same way, so using dot pitch to compare one monitor to another quickly becomes a game of "apples and oranges."

If you really want to get down to a low-level technical comparison between monitors, there are a number of good software programs you can use to test monitor performance. One of the best is the WinBench series from ZD Labs (**www.zdnet.com**). However, for many users the best way to choose one monitor over another is by performing a few simple tests in your local computer store.

Here are the tests you want to perform:

1. Start Windows (any version) and check for uniform focus. Place a few icons around the screen, in the center, in the corners, and see if they all seem to have the same clarity. Look at the vertical and horizontal lines. Are they straight or are any lines bowed? Are all the colors crisp and clear without any slight tints on any images?

2. Use a graphics program to draw a circle onscreen. Is the circle a circle or is it an oval? If you see an oval, then this monitor will cause some degree of distortion when using graphics-intensive programs.

3. Load Write or another word processing program. Type a sentence and set the font to 8-point type or smaller. Are the characters crisp and clean or are they fuzzy?

4. Turn the brightness up and down while examining the corners of the screen. Does anything change? Does the image have any swelling or blooming?

Don't immediately dismiss the monitor if it comes up short on any of these simple subjective tests. The monitor could just be connected to a lesser quality video card. See if you can get the sales representative to plug the monitor into a computer with a better card, or better yet check to see what type of return policy the computer store has in case the monitor does not perform well with your graphics card.

SETTING UP YOUR NEW MONITOR

As mentioned earlier in this lesson, a larger monitor will take up more room on your desk, so make sure that you have the available desktop real estate before you unpack your new monitor.

To set up your new monitor, do the following:

1. Turn off and unplug your current monitor. Turn off the power to your computer, and then disconnect your old monitor from your PC and remove it from your desktop.

2. Unpack your new monitor and carefully examine it for any signs of transit damage. Examine the video cable and connector, which plugs into your PC.

3. Place your new monitor on your desktop. Do not place it on top of your PC.

 Too heavy a load?   Larger monitors tend to be very heavy—too heavy in fact to place on top of your PC as many users are accustomed to doing with 14- and 15-inch monitors. Most PC cases cannot adequately support monitors weighing 50–60 pounds and could bow or crack.

4. Adjust the height of the monitor so that the approximate center of the screen is at eye level.

5. Plug your monitor's video cable into your PC and connect the power cable.

6. Turn on your monitor and your PC.

7. Your new monitor should come with a disk containing drivers for Windows 95 and Windows NT 4.0. These drivers allow Windows 95 or NT to properly adjust certain settings to those required by your monitor. Windows 3.1 does not make these adjustments. If you are using Windows 95 or NT 4.0, follow the instructions that come with your monitor for installing these drivers.

 Plug and Play ease   If you are running Windows 95 and your monitor is Plug and Play, Windows 95 will attempt to make these adjustments for you. Just follow the onscreen prompts.

 Plug and Play   This is a combination hardware and software feature that allows an operating system like Windows 95 to identify and configure hardware you add to your PC. To work, the hardware item has to have special chips built in that identify the hardware item and the operating systems, such as Windows 95, and has to be Plug and Play enabled to be able to read those chips and use the information contained within to configure the hardware.

After your monitor is correctly installed and set up, be sure to adjust the resolution to the optimum setting. If you are installing a 17-inch monitor, adjust the resolution to at least 800×600. If you have a 21-inch monitor, adjust the resolution to either 1,024×768 or 1,280×1,024. Keep in mind that these are merely suggestions for what many experts consider the optimum settings for certain size monitors. Your own preferences may dictate a higher or lower resolution. The best judge is what feels comfortable to you.

In this lesson, you learned some of what you need to know to select a new monitor. In the next lesson, you learn about modems and other communications devices.

MODEMS AND OTHER COMMUNICATIONS DEVICES

In this lesson, you learn about selecting a modem for your computer.

UNDERSTANDING MODEMS

Modem is short for ***mod**ulate **dem**odulate,* which is how a modem works to send data from one computer to another.

Modem Your computer stores data in digital form. But telephone lines transmit information as sound, which is an analog signal. The modem in your computer system converts the digital information in your computer to an analog (sound) signal and transmits the analog signal over telephone lines to another computer. The modem there converts the analog (sound) signal your computer transmitted back into a digital form.

Most standard modems today transmit data in the range of 28,800–33,600 bps (bits per second). Don't be surprised (or disappointed) if you purchase a modem advertised to operate in this range but only get transmission speeds of around 26,400 bps. Modem transmissions at higher speeds are largely governed by the quality of your telephone lines. Telephone lines for the most part are unshielded copper wire and are vulnerable to interference from a variety of sources. Interference will reduce the audio quality of the call you are making to your mother (whether you notice it or not), and interference will reduce the transmission speed of your modem as well.

Bps   Don't confuse the terms baud rate and bps (bits per second). The confusion arose years ago when modems only transmitted at 300 bps. The baud rate is the rate at which a signal between two devices changes in one second. Originally, the rate for 300 bps modems was 300 times per second, which also equals 300 baud, and so the terms were used interchangeably. Bits per second is the actual transmission speed of the data between modems. As modem speeds (bps) improved, it was not necessary (or in some cases possible) for the signaling change rate to keep pace. Now most modems transmit several bits per baud. If all this sounds complicated, just remember that the transmission speed of modems is described in terms of bits per second, not baud. A 28.8 modem is transmitting 28,800 bits per second, not 28,800 baud.

SELECTING A NEW MODEM

Modems are available in internal and external models. An internal modem (see Figure 16.1) requires a slot inside your PC. An external modem (see Figure 16.2) plugs into one of your serial ports via a serial cable.

FIGURE 16.1   An internal modem fits inside your computer, just like other devices you've learned about in this book.

FIGURE 16.2   An external modem connects to the rear of your computer.

Functionally, you will not see any differences between an internal and an external modem. In deciding which type to purchase, consider that an internal modem generally costs less than an external modem, but an internal modem will take up a slot in your PC.

INSTALLING AN INTERNAL MODEM

Installing an internal modem is fairly simple because all you have to do is insert the modem into one of your available motherboard slots and then configure your PC and/or operating system to recognize the modem.

Plug and Play   If you are running Windows 95 on your PC, make sure that any internal modem you purchase is designated Plug and Play (PnP). Plug and Play is a feature Windows 95 uses that allows the operating system to automatically detect and configure your modem to work with your PC. Plug and Play is not available in Windows 3.1 or Windows NT 4.0.

To install an internal modem, follow these steps:

1. Read the documentation that came with your modem thoroughly before you begin to install the modem.

    Check the documentation for your modem to determine whether your modem prefers to use a certain communications port (COM1, COM2). Check also to see whether you need to set any switches or jumpers for the communications port you will be using. If you have jumpers on your modem, they will be used to set your modem to use one of your two serial ports, COM1 or COM2. If you are running Windows 95 and your modem is Plug and Play, you may skip this step. If you have to set your modem by setting a jumper, make sure that you are not setting your modem to use a serial port being used by another device such as a serial mouse, or you will create a device conflict and neither device will function properly.

 Communications ports   These are connection points your computer uses for communicating with peripheral devices. Most computers have two basic types: serial and parallel. The major difference between the two types of ports is how they communicate. A parallel port transmits data 8 bits at a time. A serial port communicates 1 bit at a time. Parallel ports are typically used by your computer to communicate with printers. Serial ports are used primarily for communicating with modems and are often referred to as COM (short for communications) ports. Your computer is designed to operate with two serial ports, COM1 and COM2, but can be configured to have more.

2. Turn off your PC, remove the cover, and insert your modem into an empty slot (see Figure 16.3).

FIGURE **16.3**   Inserting an internal modem in one of your PC's slots is very similar to installing any new component on your motherboard.

3. Follow the instructions for installing any additional software that came with your modem for the operating system you are running (DOS/Windows 3.1, Windows 95, Windows NT 4.0, and so on).

INSTALLING AN EXTERNAL MODEM

External modems are even easier to install than internal modems. Just do the following:

1. Turn off your PC.

2. Plug one end of your serial cable into a serial port on the back of your PC and one end into the serial connector on your modem.

3. Turn on your PC and your modem.

4. Follow the instructions for installing any additional software that came with your modem for the operating system you are running (DOS/Windows 3.1, Windows 95, Windows NT 4.0, and so on).

WHAT ABOUT THOSE 56K MODEMS?

In the past year, 56K (56,000 bps) modems have been getting plenty of press coverage, and you are probably wondering if you should upgrade your current modem to one of the new 56K modems. For now, don't waste your money. There were two competing technologies and no real "standard" for 56K modems. But in early 1998 a standard has finally been worked out. Just make sure that you don't accidentally purchase a modem manufactured before the standard was created. Also, if you have a 56K modem, you can only communicate at 56K speeds with another computer that also has a 56K modem, and the communication link is not up to 56K speed in both directions. You can achieve a communication speed of 56K only when downloading files from the other computer. When you upload data to the other computer, your speed is only 33.6K (33,600 bps).

But perhaps the biggest reason not to waste your money on a 56K modem is that they do not achieve 56K speed in the real world. Most users report top speeds in the range of 40–45K (40,000–45,000 bps).

Although the new 56K modems can get you better communications speeds than the current batch of 28.8/33.6 modems on the market, if you are planning to purchase one for faster Internet access before a final standard is agreed upon, make sure that you check with your Internet Service provider first and purchase the same modem your ISP is using. You will get speeds greater than 28.8/33.6, but don't hold your breath waiting for a 56K connection.

ISDN

Another technology that has been around much longer than the two competing 56K technologies but continues to receive far less press coverage is ISDN.

 ISDN   Integrated Services Digital Network (ISDN) is a way of getting reliable communications speeds above 33.6K by using standard modems and using digital telephone lines instead of the analog lines used for typical phone communication. Right now ISDN gets you the most bang for your buck for connecting to the Internet.

On the plus side, ISDN works over digital telephone lines instead of your standard analog, voice-grade lines, which means that they are not susceptible to interference like analog lines. Being digital means that on an ISDN line you will always get speeds of at least 64K (or up to 128K) in both directions.

But ISDN has much on the minus side that has kept it from being widely embraced. First, you need to have a special ISDN communications line installed. Prices for ISDN have been steadily coming down over the past year or so (currently ranging between $100–$300), but prices still vary around the country and can be expensive for installation and monthly service. You also need a special ISDN interface card to access your ISDN line.

 Not a modem   ISDN interface cards are often incorrectly called ISDN modems, but they are not true modems because they do not convert a signal from digital to analog (or vice versa) as modems do.

ISDN has been extremely popular in small offices because at speeds of 128K, ISDN connections make it possible to provide Internet connections to multiple users simultaneously.

In this lesson, you learned about modems and how to install them in your PC. You also learned about newer communications technologies and how you should approach them. In the next lesson, you learn about upgrading your PC's case and power supply.

Upgrading Your PC's Case and Power Supply

In this lesson, you learn about upgrading your PC's case and power supply.

Why You Should Upgrade Your Case and Power Supply

When you purchased your current computer, it came in a perfectly good case. Everything—drives, motherboard, interface cards, and so on—was very neatly arranged and fit together in a nice, neat package. So, why would you want to snatch everything out and stuff them into a new box?

Stop for a moment, look inside your PC, and see how much room you have for adding any extra devices. Can you add one or two more hard disk drives? Can you add an internal Zip or Jaz removable disk drive? Can you add a CD-ROM drive (if you don't already have one)? Can you add a tape drive?

For whatever reason, some manufacturers use a fairly small case when they design and manufacture their PCs. Whether it is to keep the package that you place on your desk as small as possible, or whether it is to keep their costs down by keeping their package (and packaging) smaller, the end result is that you have a PC that may not be as expandable as you'd like.

Not all PCs can be upgraded to a new case   Although most PCs can be upgraded very easily into a new case, some PCs—because of their proprietary design—cannot be upgraded because their manufacturers use a non-standard motherboard and case design. If you open your PC and see a motherboard that does not seem to fit the designs mentioned in this chapter, chances are your system cannot be upgraded easily, and you should not even attempt to upgrade to a new case.

The obvious answer is to simply swap your existing case for a new one. If you read Lesson 8, "Upgrading Your System Board," then you're already aware of what it takes to replace the motherboard in your PC. To replace the case, you are placing your existing motherboard into a new case rather than placing a new motherboard in your existing case.

WHAT TO LOOK FOR IN A NEW CASE

It's not like buying a new car, but you want to look for or specify certain features when selecting a new case. Some of the features that will make your life easier include:

- *Multiple drive bays.* The main reason you are purchasing a new case is probably to add additional drives (hard disk drives, CD-ROM drives, removable media drives, and so on), so make sure your new case has more drive bays than you currently need so that you will have room to expand (see Figure 17.1). Most cases have a mixture of 3 1/2-inch and 5 1/4-inch drive bays. The 3 1/2-inch drive bays are used to add additional hard disk drives; the 5 1/4-inch bays are used for CD-ROM and removable media drives.

Buy a separate case   If you have SCSI hard disks, CD-ROM drives, or removable media drives in your PC, you can purchase a separate case to house only your drives. These SCSI cases include their own power supply and fans and are a good way to remove some of the devices responsible for some of the heat build-up in your PC.

Extra drive bays

FIGURE 17.1   This computer case has extra drive bays.

- *Multiple fans*. Keep in mind that as you add additional drives and other components, you will also be adding more heat sources in your PC. Look for cases with at least two fans, aside from the fan on the power supply. Also, look for cases with larger fans.

- *Large power supply*. In this case, large means wattage not physical girth. Try to get a power supply in the range of 250–400 watts. Keep in mind that all those additional drives you plan to add require power to operate.

- *Sturdy construction.* If you purchase locally rather than through the mail, examine the case before you buy it (be sure to examine the actual case you purchase, not just a display model). Try to get a case that seems constructed using a heavier gauge steel rather than a flimsy type of sheet metal. Look to see whether seams are even and all meet with no gaps. Check to see that the cover or door fits securely and is easy to open or remove.

- *Front panel indicators and controls.* Many cases come equipped with several front panel indicators and controls. Although all these are not essential, some can come in handy. The essential controls include a reset button, on/off switch (this prevents you from having to reach around back to turn your PC on), and a drive activity indicator light.

- *Removable mounting plate and drive bays.* A removable mounting plate (see Figure 17.2) makes it easier to install and access your motherboard and removable drive bays—both internal and external—and makes it easier to install and access any drives you install in your PC.

External drive bays   These bays hold drives that are physically accessible to you for inserting disks like floppy disk drives and CD-ROM drives. Internal drive bays hold drives that you don't need to access, such as hard disk drives.

- *Extra power connectors.* Although extra power connectors are not essential, having a few extra will save you a trip to the local computer store to purchase Y-connectors (see Figure 17.3).

FIGURE 17.2   Many tower-style cases include an easily removed mounting plate.

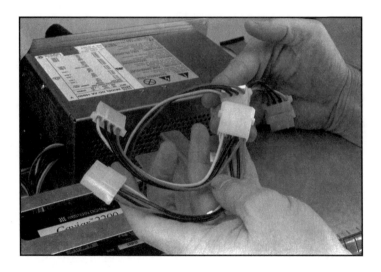

FIGURE 17.3   An extra Y-connector is a good thing to keep on hand as an extra power connector.

Cases (sometimes called chassis) that come as desktop or tower models come in a variety of sizes. Desktop case sizes are usually referred to as standard, baby AT, and slimline. Tower cases usually have a larger variety of available sizes such as mini-tower, medium, large tower, server-size, and super-sized. Usually the difference in sizes is due to the number of drive bays and the size (wattage) of the power supply.

Desktop units have the advantage of occupying a smaller piece of your office real estate and are generally less expensive than tower cases. Tower cases, on the other hand, offer more room for expansion and can be placed on the floor next to your desk so that they don't take up any valuable desktop space. When you place a tower on the floor next to your desk, you will likely have to also purchase expansion cables (longer cables) for your monitor and keyboard.

UPGRADING YOUR CASE

No hard and fast rules exist for upgrading your PC's case, but here are a few suggestions you might want to follow after you unplug the power cord, ground yourself, and remove the cover from your existing PC case:

1. Make sure you diagram where every component is located before you move anything. This includes drives, cables, power connectors, and any miscellaneous items installed in your PC.

2. Remove your interface cards first and place them in a safe location so that they will not be damaged.

3. Remove your drives and ribbon cables. Again, you should note how they are connected and what cables are connected to each drive.

4. Remove your memory and CPU. Store these in a safe location.

5. Remove your motherboard. Note any cables still attached to your motherboard and the exact placement of screws and standoffs (the small plastic support pylons under your motherboard).

You normally don't remove the power supply because almost all new cases come with power supplies already installed.

To install your components into the new case, simply follow the previous five steps in reverse order, making sure you pay close attention to your diagrams and notes.

POWER SUPPLIES

Whenever you purchase a new case, it will come equipped with a power supply. You can also purchase power supplies separately. The two main reasons for purchasing a separate power supply are

- Your existing power supply fails.

- You want to add additional devices to your PC, but your existing power supply does not output sufficient wattage.

The most important factor to consider in purchasing a new power supply is making sure it will fit in your existing case. If you do not purchase a new power supply from the same company that supplied your original power supply, then it is probably a good idea to remove the power supply you are replacing and take it with you to your local computer store. This way you can compare the new power supply to the old one. Check for size and make sure that power connection cables, mounting screws, and the off/on switch are all in the same relative positions.

 Reconnect correctly   One caution that cannot be repeated too often is the importance of making sure to properly reconnect the power supply cables to your motherboard. Make sure you note how the power supply cables are connected *before* you remove them. In most cases the two black cables are next to each other when the two connectors are plugged into the motherboard. If you accidentally reverse these connectors, you can fry your motherboard.

You can easily remove your existing power supply with just a screwdriver and a little patience. Remember to label each cable you remove, and most importantly, make sure you unplug the power supply before you begin removing it from your case.

 Don't open a failed power supply   Don't even think about trying to open a failed power supply to attempt to repair it. First, it usually isn't worth repairing. A new power supply can be purchased for around $20–$30, and second power supplies are manufactured with slow discharge capacitors that can carry a considerable (and dangerous) charge.

In this lesson, you learned about selecting and replacing your computer's case and power supply. In the next lesson, you learn about upgrading your computer's BIOS.

UPGRADING YOUR BIOS

LESSON

18

In this lesson, you learn about upgrading your PC's BIOS.

WHAT IS THE BIOS?

The next time you turn on your computer, pay close attention to the information displayed onscreen and look for the information on your PC's BIOS. The BIOS (Basic Input Output System) is software that enables your computer to boot and enables your processor to access the hardware devices, such as the hard disk drive, video card, and other peripherals. The BIOS also controls the POST—the Power On Self-Test—every time you turn on your computer.

Every BIOS is specific to a certain type of motherboard, so even if you notice that the BIOS in your computer is made by the same company that manufactures the BIOS in your neighbor's computer, it doesn't necessarily mean the BIOS in one is identical to the other. If the two of you have different makes of PC, you can almost guarantee that each BIOS is different.

WHY DO YOU NEED TO CHANGE YOUR BIOS?

Your BIOS was made about the same time as your computer, and although it may have served you well up until now, many things have changed since your computer was manufactured. New types of peripherals have been invented, disk drives have gotten larger, and new types of video cards with higher resolutions have been created, among other things. In short, the BIOS in your computer has remained static while the rest of the computer industry has continued at its usual dynamic pace. For example, the BIOS in some early model 486 computers was designed while most hard disk drives were still around 200–400MB in size. When users of these computers attempt to install newer drives in the 2–4GB range, they discover that their computers do not recognize more than 500MB of their new multigigabyte drives. The answer to this problem is simply to upgrade the BIOS.

How Do I Upgrade My BIOS?

Early 486 model computers had their BIOS stored in chips on the motherboard, which had to be physically replaced in order to upgrade the BIOS (see Figure 18.1). Later model 486 computers, however, and all computers since the first Pentium, have what are called a *flash BIOS*. This means that you can run a program on a floppy disk to upgrade your BIOS, and no physical replacement of chips is necessary.

FIGURE 18.1   BIOS chips are located on the motherboard.

How Do I Know Whether I Need to Upgrade My BIOS?

If you install a new peripheral and it doesn't work—you have checked every part of the installation procedure and everything checks out okay—then you probably need to upgrade your BIOS. Also, if you receive notice from your dealer or from your PC's manufacturer that there is a defect in your current BIOS and they recommend that you upgrade, it's time to upgrade.

How Do I Tell What Type of BIOS I Have?

If you have a Pentium or later processor in your computer, you can rest assured you have a flash BIOS. If you have a 486 processor, then the odds are even as to which type of BIOS you have. If you have the documentation that came with your PC, you can check to see whether your BIOS type is listed.

 Check the documentation If you still have the documentation listing the type of BIOS in your PC, the documentation is also likely to indicate whom to contact about upgrading your BIOS.

If you don't have the original documentation that came with your PC, turn on your PC and write down all the BIOS information displayed when your computer boots. You can also check your CMOS settings (see Lesson 5, "Understanding Your CMOS Settings") for BIOS information. After you have the BIOS information about your PC, then you can contact your PC's manufacturer to find out what type of BIOS you have. Be sure to have the model of your computer when you contact the manufacturer.

How Can I Get My BIOS Upgrade?

If you do not have a flash BIOS, you can contact your PC's manufacturer about ordering a new set of BIOS chips. You can also contact one of two BIOS upgrade companies, Micro Firmware, Inc.

and Microid Research (Unicore Software). Micro Firmware can be contacted at 800-767-5465 or 405-321-8333. You can also contact Micro Firmware at **http://www.firmware.com**. Microid Research can be reached at 800-800-BIOS and 508-686-6468. Microid's web site is located at **http://www.unicore.com** or **http://www.mrbios.com**.

If you do have a flash BIOS in your PC and you have Internet access, you can download the program to update your PC from a variety of sources. The place you should look is the web site run by your PC's manufacturer. Most computer manufacturers run a web site and provide BIOS, other upgrades, and updates for their customers.

If your PC's manufacturer does not maintain a web site, you can look on the web sites run by many of the leading BIOS manufacturers. The following is a short list of BIOS manufacturers:

- Award: **http://www.award.com**
- Phoenix: **http://www.ptltd.com**
- American Megatrends, Inc. (AMI): **http://www.megatrends.com**

You can check the company from which you purchased your PC if you did not purchase from the manufacturer. You can also check with your manufacturer or dealer if you do not have Internet access.

INSTALLING UPGRADE BIOS CHIPS

If you order BIOS upgrade chips for a computer that does not have flash BIOS, it's very easy to install the chips yourself.

To install BIOS upgrade chips, do the following:

1. Turn off and unplug your PC.

2. Discharge any static electricity by first touching the exterior of the your PC's case, and then remove the cover from your PC.

3. Examine the new BIOS upgrade chips you ordered. Notice the size of the chips and markings or labels on the chips; most importantly, look for a notch in one end of the chips (see Figure 18.2).

FIGURE 18.2   A notch on one end of the BIOS chip indicates the chip's orientation.

4. Now look on your motherboard to find chips that look similar to the chips you ordered. Record which direction the orientation notch is positioned.

5. Before you remove a chip, check your instructions to see in what position you need to replace the chips. You want to make sure that you install the replacement chips (if there is more than one chip) in the correct socket.

6. The chips you ordered should have been shipped with a tool resembling a large set of tweezers with the tips turned inward. This tool is a chip extractor, or chip puller. You should have also received instructions on how to use the chip extractor to remove your old BIOS chips. If the

instructions are not included, simply place each of the turned in tips under the ends (length-wise) of the chips and gently lift upward, rocking back and forth, until the chip lifts out of its socket. Repeat this procedure for all your old BIOS chips. If a chip extractor did not come with your new BIOS chips, a trip to your local computer store can usually remedy this oversight.

No chip extractor? If you don't have a chip extractor, you can also remove your chip by gently prying it out using a small flatblade screwdriver. Just make sure to pry one side and then the other, a little at a time, until each chip is loose enough to remove. Keep in mind, however, that a chip extractor is the safest and preferred method of removing chips.

7. Replace your old chips with the new chips you ordered. Make sure you insert the chips with the orientation notch facing in the same direction as the chips you just removed. Be very careful not to accidentally bend any of the pins on the chips as you insert them into their sockets. If the pins on a chip are spread too far apart, place the chip on its side on a hard surface like a tabletop and gently roll the pins until they are a little closer. By placing the chip on its side and rolling it, you make sure you bend all the pins evenly.

8. Double-check your work to make sure that the new chips are properly installed in their sockets, that they are oriented properly, and that no pins are bent. When everything looks okay, turn on your PC. If the new BIOS chips are properly installed, your PC should boot as before. If you need to rerun your hardware Setup program, do so and reenter any information your PC requests.

UPGRADING A FLASH **BIOS**

Upgrading a PC with flash BIOS is a snap. If you ordered the BIOS upgrade program from the manufacturer or your dealer, the program should come on a bootable disk. If you downloaded the BIOS upgrade program from the manufacturer's bulletin board or web site, follow the instructions to create a bootable upgrade disk.

To upgrade your flash BIOS, follow these steps:

1. Turn off your PC.

2. Place your BIOS upgrade disk into your floppy disk drive and turn on your PC.

3. The bootable disk should run and automatically upgrade your flash BIOS. Watch your screen for any prompts asking you to enter any information about your PC. The entire upgrade procedure should take about 1–3 minutes.

4. When the upgrade is completed, remove the upgrade disk and reboot your PC.

In this lesson, you learned about your PC's BIOS and what you need to do to upgrade your BIOS. In the next lesson, you learn about upgrading your PC's sound system.

19

Upgrading Your PC's Sound System

In this lesson, you learn about selecting a sound card and speakers for your PC.

Your Current Sound System

In the past year or so, many PC manufacturers have been delivering so-called multimedia systems complete with high-resolution video systems, CD-ROM drives, sound cards, and speakers. Although these systems, targeted mainly at home users, are capable of delivering vivid graphics, dazzling animation, and thundering sound, they are still clearly in the minority. Most PCs sold today go to corporations for general business use, and although many have multimedia capabilities, most PCs are sadly lacking many of the key ingredients, especially decent sound systems.

Most PCs sold today have a sound system no better than what was placed into the original IBM PCs sold back in 1981. Look inside your PC, and you likely will see a pitiful 5.5cm speaker, which is barely capable of producing a few odd beeps and chirps. But don't be too quick to criticize the continuing state of PC sound. The vast majority of software created for the PC in the past 16 years has made few demands on a PC's sound system.

If you did not purchase a multimedia-equipped PC, don't despair. By the end of this lesson, you will have all the information you need to turn your PC into a sound machine.

Selecting a Sound Card

Sound card usage basically falls into two camps—those users who mainly use their sound cards to listen to prerecorded audio in the form of games and CDs, and those users who install additional equipment for creating their own computer-generated audio. The vast majority of users fall into the first camp, which is the one we concentrate on in this lesson.

If the most you plan to do with audio capability is listen to music and sound that someone else has recorded (such as audio tracks on games and educational CD-ROMs, or the occasional Duke Ellington music CD), then you need to understand that most of the audio computer world is Sound Blaster–compatible (see Figure 19.1).

Music CDs   You don't really need a sound card that is Sound Blaster–compatible to listen to music CDs. In fact, you don't even need a sound card of any type in your PC to listen to music CDs. Virtually all CD-ROM players today include a headphone jack that you can plug into with a set of headphones and listen contentedly for hours. If you want to hear booming bass drums, however, you likely will want to channel your audio through a sound card and out to a good set of speakers—for that, *any* sound card suffices.

Sound Blaster sound cards currently have the lion's share of the computer audio market, a dominance that grew largely out of its early adoption by the computer gaming industry as its standard and the Sound Blaster's early compatibility with the AdLib (a pre-Sound Blaster model) sound card.

Some of the earliest Sound Blaster cards weren't really good for much except games, which really wasn't a problem for most computer users because games comprised better than 90 percent of all software with any type of sound or audio track. Today, however, Sound Blaster sound cards are considered by some to be near the top of the line for both games and serious music composition using MIDI devices and synthesizers.

FIGURE 19.1   A Sound Blaster sound card kit enables you to add speakers to your system.

 MIDI   The Musical Instrument Digital Interface is an interface and a file format that enables you to connect a musical instrument to a computer and store musical instrument data. The musical instrument data can then be edited and played back.

If you purchase a Sound Blaster sound card or compatible card, you should not have any trouble playing any type of computer audio file that you encounter.

Compatability guaranteed? Just remember the old computer maxim, "Compatibility is in the eyes of the beholder." Although some sound cards may claim to be Sound Blaster–compatible, there is no absolute guarantee.

SELECTING SPEAKERS

Selecting speakers is largely a matter of what your budget can afford. In general, the old saying "you get what you pay for" applies. Just make certain that you purchase speakers designed for use with computers, because these speakers are shielded to prevent the magnetic coils in the speakers from causing distortion or damaging your monitor should you choose to place the speakers next to your monitor. Most computer stores that sell speakers have some sort of display enabling you to compare one model against another. Before you purchase, try to decide what type of audio you will be listening to. Will you mostly be playing games with your PC, or will you mostly use your sound card and speakers to listen to relaxing music CDs while you work? Having an idea of what type of audio your speakers will be used for can help you to decide how much you want to spend.

INSTALLING A SOUND CARD AND SPEAKERS

Little setup is needed to install a sound card in your PC. The sound card comes preconfigured with its default settings, which works well in most PCs. If your sound card does not work after you complete the installation, one of the settings might be conflicting with another device already using that setting in your PC. The most common problem occurs if one of your sound card's default settings uses the same interrupt request (IRQ) that another device in your PC is already using. If so, simply follow the instructions that accompany your sound card for changing the interrupt request used by the sound card. Usually changing an interrupt on a sound card is accomplished by running a Setup program for it. (See Lesson 3, "Examining Your Current PC," for more information on your IRQ settings.)

To install a sound card, follow these steps:

1. Read all the installation instructions that come with your sound card. In addition to instructions for installation, you often see cautions or warnings about potential problems that other users may have encountered.

2. Turn off and unplug your PC. Ground yourself and then remove the cover.

3. Locate a vacant slot on your motherboard where you can install the sound card.

4. Insert the sound card into the slot (see Figure 19.2).

Figure 19.2 Inserting a sound card into an empty slot in your computer is much like installing any other type of card.

5. If you have a CD-ROM drive installed in your PC, attach the audio cable from the audio connector on the sound card to the audio connector on the back of the CD-ROM

drive. You may have to remove your CD-ROM drive to access the audio connector.

6. Plug in your speakers according to the instructions that accompany your speakers. The speakers plug into the connector labeled **audio out** or **speakers** on the back of your sound card (see Figure 19.3).

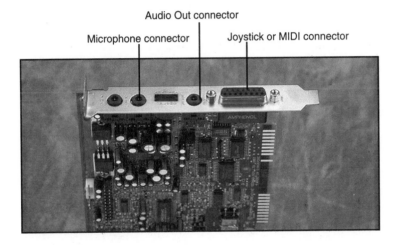

FIGURE 19.3   The connectors on a typical sound card include a microphone jack, audio out connector, and a joystick or MIDI connector.

7. Replace your PC's cover and turn on your PC.

8. Depending on which operating system you are using on your PC, you might have to run software to configure your operating system so that it recognizes your new sound card. If you are running Windows 95 and your new sound card is designed as Plug and Play, Windows 95 should automatically recognize your sound card and begin the configuration process for you. If this happens, just follow the onscreen prompts to complete the configuration.

When you complete the configuration process, the configuration software should include a procedure to test your newly installed sound card. Make sure the speakers you attached are plugged in to the correct connector and that they are turned on. If the audio test fails, review the instructions for your sound card, and make sure you followed each step correctly. If you still can't find the cause of the problem, rerun the PC checklist program from Lesson 3 and check the interrupt settings to make sure your sound card is not in conflict with another device in your PC. After you have uncovered and resolved the problem, retest your sound card and enjoy the new dimension you've just added to your PC.

In this lesson, you learned how to install a sound card and speakers in your PC. In the next lesson, you learn how to select and install a printer.

Selecting and Installing Your Printer

20

*In this lesson, you learn about
selecting a printer and how to set up your printer to work with your PC.*

Types of Printers

All printers fall into one of two broad categories—impact or non-impact printers. *Impact printers* employ some type of mechanical process to form characters or images by physically striking (or impacting) paper or some other printable medium. Some examples of impact printers are:

- Dot-matrix
- Daisy-wheel

Non-impact printers use a non-physical (or non-impact) process to transfer characters or an image to paper. Some examples of non-impact printers are:

- Laser
- Inkjet
- Thermal

A few years ago, dot-matrix printers reigned supreme due primarily to their speed and the fact that they were relatively inexpensive. Some of the better dot-matrix printers could also produce what was then called "near letter-quality" text.

Today, however, dot-matrix printers have declined in popularity now that laser and inkjet printers have dropped dramatically in price and have made true typeset-quality and color text affordable.

SELECTING A PRINTER

For many users, price is ultimately the deciding factor in choosing between purchasing a laser or inkjet printer. Laser printers (see Figure 20.1) are still more expensive to purchase but cheaper to operate than inkjet printers. Inkjet printers (see Figure 20.2) are less expensive but still command a higher per-page cost to operate. Laser printers still average about one-half cent per page, whereas inkjet printers can range anywhere from about 2–10 cents per page. It doesn't sound like much initially, until you begin to multiply these costs by several hundred or several thousand pages.

FIGURE 20.1   A laser printer. *(Photo courtesy of Epson America.)*

But price should be only one of several factors you use in deciding what type of printer is best for your needs. In addition to price, other factors you should consider before purchasing a printer are:

- Print speed
- Print quality
- Color versus monochrome
- Availability of printer drivers

FIGURE 20.2   An inkjet printer. *(Photo courtesy of Hewlett-Packard.)*

PRINT SPEED

Laser printers still lead the race over the inkjet when it comes to churning out pages per minute, but the inkjet is rapidly closing the gap. Most personal laser printers print in the 6-8 ppm (pages per minute) range, whereas many inkjet printers can print mono-chrome text (one color text, usually black) in the 4-6 ppm range.

PRINT QUALITY

Print quality is measured by resolution, similar to video resolution. You'll remember from Lesson 14, "Upgrading Your Video Card," that video resolution is measured by pixels (picture elements) on the entire screen measured horizontally and vertically (for example, 640×480, 800×600). Printer resolution is also measured horizontally and vertically, but instead of the entire screen or page, the resolution is measured within a one-inch (1 by 1 inch) square. Instead of pixels, printer resolution is measured in dots per inch (dpi). For example, most laser printers now print at a resolution of 600×600 dpi.

Dots per inch The "dots per inch" resolution of a printer should be described using both the horizontal and vertical measurements (600×600 dpi) but often, if the measurements are the same, the description will be shortened. For example, a resolution of 300×300 dpi will be shortened to simply 300 dpi. Therefore, when you see the common resolution of 600 dpi, you will know that the resolution is in fact 600×600 dpi.

Although most laser printers seem to have standardized on a resolution of 600×600 dpi, inkjet printers run the gamut from about 600×300 dpi to 720×1440 dpi. When printing text, laser printers seem to still have a slight edge over inkjet printers. However, when printing graphic images many inkjet printers can produce much higher quality printouts than laser printers.

High-resolution laser printers (1200×1200 dpi) are available that can produce camera-ready output, but these are priced in the $5,000 range and are usually used only by graphics professionals.

If you use dpi as one of your determining factors in purchasing a printer, consider these suggestions. For printing text such as letters or manuscripts, 300 dpi is adequate. Most users will not be able to distinguish text printed at 300 dpi and text printed at 600 dpi. When printing graphics, however, higher resolution usually means a better quality print. Most users will be able to distinguish a graphic image printed at 300 dpi and the same image printed at 600 dpi.

Color Versus Monochrome

Here the decision is usually much simpler. If you need to print in color, you need an inkjet. If you are satisfied with printing only in black and white, get a laser printer.

Have money to burn?   Color laser printers are available, but unfortunately they are still in the $2,000–$3,000 and up price range. Most users who require color still opt for inkjet printers, which can produce output at nearly the quality of color laser printers, and at a fraction of the cost.

Keep in mind that with an inkjet printer you can also choose to print in just black and white. Many inkjet users will produce draft copies of their output in black and white, and then print the final output in color.

AVAILABILITY OF PRINTER DRIVERS

Most printer manufacturers are targeting Windows 95 users. If you are running Windows 95, you should not have a problem getting nearly any laser and inkjet printer on the market to work with your PC. Most manufacturers are also still producing drivers for use with Windows 3.1, and many are also producing drivers for Windows NT.

Get the correct print drivers   Before you purchase a printer, check with the manufacturer or your sales rep to make sure that drivers are available for the operating system you are using.

INSTALLING YOUR PRINTER

Printers are among the easiest peripherals to install, especially if you are running Windows 95. Most printers today are designed to connect to your PC via the parallel port, so basically all you need to connect your PC and printer is a standard Centronics parallel cable.

Centronics parallel cable   This is a simple communications cable with a 36-pin Centronics connector on one end and a 25-pin female connector on the other end. You can purchase a Centronics parallel cable in most computer stores in lengths ranging from 6 to 15 feet. And don't believe that myth about parallel cables having to be less than 10 feet in length. If you need a 15-foot cable, go ahead and purchase one. Many stores now carry printer cables in lengths of 25 and even 50 feet.

CONNECTING YOUR PRINTER

To connect your printer to your PC, perform the following steps:

1. Unpack and set up your printer according to the manufacturer's instructions.

2. Take your parallel cable and plug the 36-pin Centronics connector into the parallel port on your printer (see Figure 20.3).

FIGURE 20.3   A Centronics parallel connector on a printer.

3. Plug the other end of your printer cable (the end with the 25-pin female connector) into the parallel port on the back of your PC. If you're not sure which port is the parallel port, refer to Lesson 2.

4. Turn on your PC and your printer.

INSTALLING YOUR PRINTER DRIVER WITH WINDOWS 95

If you are running Windows 95, the installation of your printer driver should begin as soon as Windows 95 is restarted, provided your printer is designed as a Plug and Play peripheral. Simply follow the onscreen prompts and insert the printer driver disk when instructed.

 Printer drivers Before you can use your printer, you need to install the appropriate printer driver. A printer driver is simply a small program that allows your PC to communicate with your printer.

If Windows 95 does not automatically begin installing your printer driver, follow these steps to start the driver installation:

1. Select **Start** to open the Start menu.

2. Select **Settings** and **Printers** to open the Windows 95 Printer Control section (see Figure 20.4).

FIGURE 20.4 The Windows 95 printer control section.

3. Double-click **Add Printer** to start the Add Printer Wizard (see Figure 20.5) and follow the prompts to install your printer driver.

FIGURE 20.5   The Windows 95 Add Printer Wizard.

INSTALLING YOUR PRINTER DRIVER WITH WINDOWS 3.1

If you are running Windows 3.1, follow the instructions accompanying your printer to install your printer driver. In most cases, you will need to insert your driver disk and run the driver installation program.

INSTALLING YOUR PRINTER DRIVER UNDER WINDOWS NT

Installing a printer driver under Windows NT is very similar to installing the printer driver under Windows 95. Unlike Windows 95, Windows NT will not automatically recognize Plug and Play peripherals, so you'll need to perform the same steps to manually start the NT Add Printer Wizard from the Start menu.

Installing a Second Printer to Your PC

So far, we have discussed how to install only one printer to your PC. But what if you have one PC but need to connect two printers? It's not uncommon for many users to have both a laser and an inkjet printer. The remaining section of this lesson tells you how you can connect both to your PC.

You can connect two printers to your PC in three different ways:

- You can set up the second printer next to the first printer and switch the printer cable from one printer to the other.

- You can purchase and install a second parallel port in your PC and connect the second printer to this second port using a second printer cable.

- You can purchase a device called an A/B switch and use it to switch the communication signal from one printer to the other.

 Connect to a serial port   A fourth possible solution might be to connect one printer to a parallel port and connect the other printer to one of your serial ports. This solution is less advisable than the three previously mentioned because not all printers sold today can be connected using a serial port. Another possible problem with using a serial port is that serial cables are not nearly as standardized as parallel cables, and you might have some difficulty locating a serial cable that will work with your printer.

Unplugging the Cable

To connect two printers to one PC, switching the printer is the easiest—but not necessarily the most convenient—way to go. You simply install drivers for both printers, and when you want to switch from one printer to the other you unplug the cable from the back of one printer and plug the cable into the parallel port of the other printer.

Choose the correct driver   Regardless of which of the three possible solutions you choose, remember that you need to select the appropriate driver in Windows. In most Windows applications, you can select a different printer driver from the Print dialog box.

Installing a Second Parallel Port

Installing a second parallel port in your PC for a second printer is perhaps the most convenient of the three solutions. A second parallel port can be purchased on an interface card from most computer stores for $35 or less and installed in less than 10 minutes.

Keep your ports straight   Sometimes the interface card you purchase for your second parallel port might contain one or two additional serial ports as well. To prevent any possible conflicts with your existing serial ports, simply follow the instructions with the card to disable the two serial ports.

If you purchase a second parallel port, you need to check a few settings on the interface card before you install it in your PC. First, make sure that the parallel port on the interface card is set to function as LPT2 and not set to function as LPT1. The parallel port in your PC is set to function as LPT1 by default. If both ports are set to LPT1, the two ports are likely to conflict and not allow you to print.

You also need to check the memory address and the interrupt request (IRQ) the parallel port on the interface card is set to use to make sure they are not in conflict with the memory address and interrupt used by the parallel port in your PC. Use the PC Dr. program you used in Lesson 3 to check the memory address and interrupt in use by the parallel port in your PC. (The interrupt most likely will be 7 because this is usually the default interrupt used for LPT1. The memory address will look something like 3BC or 2BC. Just make sure that you check which settings your existing parallel port uses.)

 Check the card settings   Many manufacturers understand that a parallel port on an interface card will be installed as a second parallel port and will attempt to set the configuration of the parallel port so it will not conflict with the usual settings for LPT1. Check the documentation that comes with the card to see how the card was set at the factory.

To install the interface card, follow these steps:

1. Turn off and unplug your PC. Ground yourself and then remove the cover.

2. Insert the interface card in an empty slot in your PC.

3. Replace the cover and turn on your PC.

4. Run your PC's hardware Setup program and install or enable LPT2. If you have to include the interrupt and memory address in the setup, enter the settings the same as they are on the card.

You now can connect the second printer just the same as you connected the first printer earlier in this lesson.

INSTALLING AN A/B SWITCH

An A/B switch is like a fork in the road—it allows you to travel in one of two directions. In this case, the A/B switch is a device that allows the signal from your PC to travel to one of two printers.

Essentially, the A/B switch is a device or electrical connector box with one cable attached to your PC and two cables attached to each of your two printers. The device is called an A/B switch because a switch allows you to select printer A or printer B.

The A/B switch is just a hardware device, meaning that there is no setup program to run. To install, just plug one cable from your PC in to the input port on the switch. You then connect the remaining two cables from each output port to each of your printers. Now when you want to print to the printer connected to the first output port, you move the selector on the switch to the A position. When you want to print to the printer connected to the second output port, you move the selector on the switch to the B position. The biggest problem in using an A/B switch is making sure that you get the input and output cable installed correctly. But most A/B switches usually ship with more than enough documentation to walk you through the connections. An estimate on the price of an A/B switch is anywhere from $35 to $75.

In this lesson, you learned how to set up a printer to work with your PC. In the next lesson, you learn how to set up and use a scanner and a few tips on using a digital camera.

Scanners and Digital Cameras

*In this lesson, you learn about select-
ing a scanner and a digital camera and how to use them with your PC.*

Scanners

For home use, you can choose from basically three types of scanners—flatbed, handheld, and sheetfeed scanners. Handheld scanners were designed basically for computer users with very limited
funds to devote to a scanning device. Because sheetfeed scanners
were developed and because prices for flatbed scanners have been
dropping steadily, it's likely handheld scanners will all but disappear very shortly. No one recommends purchasing a handheld
scanner because the images produced by handheld scanners are
almost always distorted—it is nearly impossible to move the scanner over the object you are scanning at a constant speed. Although there are three types you can still purchase for home use,
my recommendation for a home scanner limits your selection to
just two types—flatbed and sheetfeed models.

Sheetfeed Scanners

Sheetfeed scanners are the less expensive of the two types recommended and have virtually replaced handheld scanners as the
low-end model.

Besides being less expensive than flatbed scanners, one major
advantage sheetfeed scanners have is that they occupy much less
desktop space. The typical flatbed scanner takes up a desktop area
approximately 14 by 20 inches, whereas the typical sheetfeed
scanner only takes up an area approximately 12 by 4 inches (see
Figure 21.1).

FIGURE 21.1   A typical sheetfeed scanner.

Although sheetfeed scanners are capable of scanning pictures and converting them to digital images, most users who purchase sheetfeed scanners use them for Optical Character Recognition (OCR).

Optical Character Recognition (OCR)   A means of using your scanner and special software to scan a page of text like a newspaper or magazine article and convert what is being scanned into a text file. Some OCR programs can also convert the scanned document into several popular word processing formats, such as Microsoft Word and Corel WordPerfect.

Sheetfeed scanners can scan pictures and photos and convert them to digital images, but most sheetfeed scanners have a lower optical resolution than their flatbed siblings. Most sheetfeed scanners have a maximum optical resolution of 300×600 dpi (dots per inch).

Dots per inch   Just like printers measure their output in dots per inch (see Lesson 20, "Selecting and Installing Your Printer"), scanners measure their input in terms of dots per inch, also.

 Check optical resolution   Scanner manufacturers will often present resolution in two sets of numbers. They will list the maximum optical resolution and they will list a higher resolution value called the "interpolated" resolution. Interpolation is a means of "guessing" certain color values during the scanning process. Interpolation values can in some cases be fairly accurate. Nevertheless, you should never rely on the interpolated resolution as the maximum resolution your scanner is capable of achieving. Always use the optical resolution when comparing resolutions between scanner models.

FLATBED SCANNERS

Of the two types of scanners recommended here, flatbed models (see Figure 21.2) are the more versatile because they allow you to scan single sheets or photos. You can also place larger, bulkier objects like books and magazines on the flatbed for scanning. On many models of flatbed scanners, you can attach optional sheet feeders for scanning multipage documents.

Flatbed scanners also tend to have a slightly higher optical scanning resolution. Most home-use flatbed scanners have an optical resolution of 600×600 dpi.

FIGURE 21.2   A typical flatbed scanner. *(Photo courtesy of UMAX.)*

SELECTING A SCANNER

Now that you know about the types of scanner available, it might be helpful to provide you with a few helpful hints on how to select a scanner.

First, decide what you want to do with your scanner. If you just plan to scan a few documents and occasionally scan a few family photos, you can probably get by with a sheetfeed scanner. If you need a scanner for doing a lot of document scanning, however, then you will probably do better with a flatbed scanner with an optional sheet feeder.

If you need to scan pictures, photos, or artwork for direct transfer to a web site, then you can probably be satisfied with a sheetfeed scanner. But if you need to scan pictures, photos, or artwork, and you plan to use some type of digital editing software on the scanned image—such as Adobe Photoshop, CorelDRAW 8, or Paint Shop Pro—then you will probably need the slightly higher optical resolution offered by a flatbed scanner.

Keep in mind how much scanning you plan to do. If you will be doing a lot of scanning, you will probably want to purchase a scanner with a SCSI interface (see Lesson 9, "Hard Disk Upgrades," for more information on SCSI interfaces) because a SCSI interface will be faster than a parallel or serial interface.

Shop around Although this may begin to sound like a broken record, before you purchase any peripheral check several of the major PC journals for product reviews. It's not difficult to find a product review on scanners every other month or so, especially with the abundance of lower priced scanners coming onto the market in recent months.

INSTALLING YOUR SCANNER

A year ago it was next to impossible to purchase a scanner that did not use a SCSI interface. Now you can purchase scanners that connect to your PC using either a SCSI, parallel, or serial interface.

Avoid proprietary interface card A few scanner manufacturers still use a proprietary interface and supply their scanners with a proprietary interface card. Most experts, myself included, recommend against any device utilizing a proprietary interface because they usually offer no significant advantage over other available interfaces, and they take up space in your PC that cannot by used by other devices.

Use SCSI for speed Of the three available interfaces for scanners, a SCSI interface will deliver the fastest performance. The parallel port interface is next, and the serial interface is the slowest.

Because scanners are external devices, you connect them to your PC much the same as you would connect a printer. To install your scanner, follow these steps:

1. Unpack and set up your scanner following the instructions supplied by the manufacturer.

2. If you need to install an interface card for your scanner, turn off your PC, ground yourself, remove the cover, locate an empty slot, and install the interface card into the empty slot.

 Some scanner manufacturers include a SCSI card with their scanners, eliminating the need to purchase a SCSI card if you don't already have one. Sometimes, however, these supplied SCSI cards are designed to work only with the scanner they are shipped with and will not function with other SCSI devices.

3. Connect your scanner to your PC using the cable shipped with your scanner. Follow the manufacturer's instructions.

 Cable included   Virtually every scanner manufacturer supplies a cable with their scanner.

4. Insert the disk supplied with your scanner and follow the instructions to install the scanner software. The scanner software consists of the hardware driver needed to allow your PC to communicate with your scanner and usually also several utility programs supplied by the manufacturer.

DIGITAL CAMERAS

If you are interested in scanning photos and creating digital images, a digital camera will save you the scanning step. A digital camera is just what the name suggests — a photographic camera that produces digital images. A digital camera (see Figure 21.3) does not use film. Instead, a digital camera contains memory where images are stored until you download them to your PC.

FIGURE 21.3   A typical digital camera. *(Photo courtesy of Epson America.)*

A digital camera is highly convenient—especially when you consider that your images are almost immediately available for use and you don't have to stop to have your film developed. Nevertheless, digital cameras do have their drawbacks:

- Digital cameras are still expensive. A good digital camera costs about $1,000. Lesser quality digital cameras can be purchased for around $300-500.

- Digital cameras cannot produce images at the same quality of standard film cameras. Even a moderately priced 35mm film camera can produce photos superior to digital cameras because film can produce images with a much higher resolution than the best digital cameras.

With these negatives, you might wonder why anyone would ever bother with a digital camera. The primary reason is convenience.

The primary uses of digital cameras are in areas where the lower resolution produced by digital cameras is not a problem, namely Web-based graphics. Because Web-based graphics do not need to be any greater than 75 dpi, the convenience offered by digital cameras makes producing Web-based graphics a cinch.

SELECTING A DIGITAL CAMERA

Digital cameras can range in price from a few hundred dollars to several thousand dollars. But don't get the impression that you can't get a usable digital camera without taking out a second mortgage. There are several dozen very good digital cameras priced in the $300-800 range. Just like every other product mentioned in this book, you need to check the popular PC journals for product reviews to get an idea how the various models of digital cameras in your price range compare. Just like scanners, the quality of digital cameras can vary considerably for models in the same price range. You also need to be aware of what add-on products are available for various digital cameras. Some cameras allow you to add additional memory to boost the number of photos you can take before you have to download images to your PC. Some cameras come equipped with the same type of peripheral slots found on laptop computers and allow you to use the same memory and hard disk peripherals available for laptop computers.

In this lesson, you learned how to set up a scanner to work with your PC and how to select and use a digital camera. In the next lesson, you learn the hows and whys of upgrading to a new operating system.

Upgrading to a New Operating System

In this lesson, you learn about upgrading your PC's operating system.

Limitations of DOS/Windows 3.1

If you are still using DOS, you are using an operating system that has been around in some form since 1981. Without going through the history or evolution of DOS, its biggest limitations include

- DOS was essentially written for the 80286 processor, which means DOS cannot address more than 16MB of memory for program execution.

- DOS lacks any type of system or file security.

- DOS uses the 8.3 filename convention (the filename can be 1–8 characters and the file extension can be 1–3 characters).

- DOS uses the FAT16 formatting structure for formatting hard disks, which means DOS cannot create hard disk partitions larger than 2GB.

- DOS is a single-tasking operating system, which means you can only run one program at a time.

Windows 3.1 is an operating environment—not an operating system—that resides on top of DOS and maintains most of the DOS limitations. Windows 3.1 was written to work on an 80386 processor. Perhaps the biggest reason to upgrade from Windows 3.1 is that software is no longer being developed for it.

Now you're probably thinking, I'm using Windows 3.1, I surf the Net, and I use the latest versions of Netscape and Internet Explorer, so what do you mean software isn't being developed for Windows 3.1? The versions of Netscape and Internet Explorer you're using were developed for Windows 95 and NT, and the Windows 3.1 versions that you're using are scaled back versions created for people who have not upgraded yet. The versions you're using are not functionally equivalent to the Windows 95 and NT versions.

Let's use the Internet to further illustrate the limitations of Windows 3.1. One of the premier World Wide Web animation tools is a program called Shockwave by Macromedia. Go to the Macromedia web site at **http://www.macromedia.com** and see whether you can download a version of the Shockwave ActiveX control viewer for Windows 3.1. Go to a few other sites and see how many programs, plug-ins, and utilities are available only for Windows 95/NT or are available in a scaled down version for Windows 3.1. A few of them are

- **http://www.realaudio.com**
- **http://www.tucows.com**
- **http://www.download.com**
- **http://www.shareware.com**

Do you need more convincing? In late 1997, Microsoft announced it was no longer selling Windows 3.1. This announcement officially makes Windows 3.1 obsolete.

WHY YOU SHOULD UPGRADE

I've told you why you should stop using Windows 3.1. Now I'll tell you why you should upgrade to either Windows 95 or NT. If you are considering an upgrade from Windows 3.1, you can set aside your number one fear; all your existing software will run under Windows 95 or NT. You do not have to junk all your current programs and buy new ones. In fact, the main reason you should upgrade from Windows 3.1 to Windows 95 or NT is that your existing programs actually run better. One major advantage Windows 95 and NT have over Windows 3.1 is their greater capability to manage usage of your computer's memory. Memory usage problems caused frequent system crashes in Windows 3.1.

If you are an active Windows 3.1 user, you undoubtedly have experienced the dreaded GPF—General Protection Fault. A GPF occurs when Windows 3.1 attempts to enable two programs to use the same area of memory. GPFs do not exist in Windows 95 or NT because both manage memory usage so well.

Windows NT offers the best crash protection This is not to say that Windows 95 and Windows NT will never crash because of errant programs. But if you are looking for crash protection, Windows NT has the best. In Windows NT, a problem with one program does not affect the performance of another program. If a program crashes under NT, only that program is affected, and NT enables you to gracefully shut down the bothersome program (and then restart it if you like) without affecting the rest of your work. How many of you Windows 3.1 users have lost hours of unsaved work because another program you had open crashed and brought down the entire system?

Both Windows 95 and NT come with all the tools you need to access the Internet. No extra programs or utilities are necessary to access the Internet. Of course, you can purchase or download other programs, but Windows 95 and NT enable you to access the Internet right out of the box (provided you have an Internet connection).

Perhaps the best reason to upgrade to either Windows 95 or NT, however, is upgrading to a true multitasking operating system.

Multitasking This means that several programs or tasks can run simultaneously. In Windows 95 and NT, the operating system controls the amount of CPU time allotted to each running procedure or application.

Some of the pluses and minuses of Windows 3.1 versus Windows 95/NT are

- Windows 3.1 is single-tasking; Windows 95/NT are multitasking.

- Windows 3.1 has very limited memory management. Windows 95/NT have extensive memory management.

- Windows 3.1 has no file or system security. Windows 95 has minimal system security. Windows NT has extensive file and system security.

- Windows 3.1 runs your existing (16-bit) applications. Windows 95/NT runs your existing (16-bit) applications and the more advanced 32-bit applications.

- Windows 3.1 is not designed to efficiently handle large disk drives. Windows 95/NT are both designed to manage large drives and large partitions.

- Windows 3.1 does not include applications or utilities for accessing the Internet. Windows 95/NT both include utilities and applications for accessing the Internet.

WINDOWS 95 OR WINDOWS NT 4.0

So, to which operating system should you upgrade—Windows 95 or Windows NT? Well, it depends on what you need a new operating system for, what you intend to do with your new operating system, what your level of computer experience is, and the speed of your PC's processor. Right now, Microsoft is marketing Windows 95 as the operating system for most home users and Windows NT for the corporate workplace. Windows NT does require a PC with a little more processing speed, but in return for that extra bit of power, Windows NT gives you better memory management, better crash protection, and better security than Windows 95. Windows NT is also a little more complex and a little more difficult to learn and use than Windows 95.

If you are planning to upgrade your home computer, you're probably better off upgrading to Windows 95 because the needs and demands of home users typically are not as pressing as those of the user in the corporate environment.

UPGRADING TO WINDOWS 95

Unfortunately, Microsoft did not provide a clear upgrade path from Windows 3.1 to Windows 95. Although it is possible to install Windows 95 on top of an existing installation of Windows 3.1, my advice is: don't! The installation of Windows 95 will not be done cleanly because many Windows 3.1 files are left on your hard disk during the installation that can potentially interact with similar Windows 95 files and be a potential source of problems. For best results, back up all your existing data files, delete Windows 3.1 entirely from your hard disk drive (delete the C:\WINDOWS directory), and then install Windows 95. Afterwards, reinstall all your existing software applications. This procedure takes a little longer than installing Windows 95 on top of Windows 3.1, but you are better off in the long run.

Make sure also that you have upgraded the memory in your PC. The minimum amount of memory you should have for Windows 95 is 16MB, but you'll find that Windows 95 performs best for most home users if your PC has 24MB to 32MB of RAM.

UPGRADING TO WINDOWS NT

Upgrading from Windows 3.1 to Windows NT is a little different from upgrading to Windows 95. Although there is still no clear cut upgrade path, Windows NT is a little more accommodating to a previous installation of Windows 3.1 than is Windows 95. Windows NT comes with a dual-boot utility that enables you, after the

NT installation, to boot either Windows 3.1 or NT provided that you install Windows NT into a different directory than the one in which you earlier installed Windows 3.1.

My recommendation for installing Windows NT is that you install it into a different directory than the one in which you installed Windows 3.1. For example, Windows 3.1 is typically installed into the C:\WINDOWS directory and Windows NT is typically installed into a C:\WINNT directory. This installation decision along with NT's dual-boot utility effectively enables you to continue using both systems on your PC, although not at the same time.

It's also recommended that you not attempt to run Windows NT unless you have at least a Pentium 100 MHz processor in your PC. NT runs with a lesser processor, but you will not be happy with the performance.

Although Windows NT performs on PCs with 16MB of RAM, most users find that performance is a little sluggish. Windows NT performs best with at least 32MB of RAM, and if you can install 64MB, you will enjoy excellent performance.

In this lesson, you learned about upgrading your operating system and some of the considerations you must use in deciding between Windows 95 and Windows NT. In the next lesson, you learn about some additional performance monitors and diagnostic tools that you can use to help troubleshoot problems on your PC.

PERFORMANCE MONITORS AND DIAGNOSTIC TOOLS

In this lesson, you learn about using PC performance monitoring and diagnostic tools.

IDENTIFYING NEW TOOLS

In Lesson 3, "Examining Your Current PC," you learned about using diagnostic utilities to analyze your PC. In this lesson you are introduced to a few additional utilities that you can use to analyze your PC, monitor system performance, and diagnose problems with your system. Some of the utilities shown here are commercial products; others are available free (or for a minimal shareware registration fee).

NORTON UTILITIES

The granddaddy of PC utilities is the collection of programs known as the Norton Utilities. Originally created by Peter Norton for the original IBM PC back in the early 1980s, the early versions of the Norton Utilities were mainly for file repair and recovery with a few odd (minimal) analysis and diagnostic utilities thrown in for good measure. The Norton Utilities have evolved and grown with PCs for the last decade and a half and now feature an extensive array of utilities to monitor your PC for potential problems. The Norton Utilities are currently available in versions for both Windows 95 and Windows NT. Of the two versions, the Windows 95 version is the more complete (not all the utilities originally created to operate in the Windows 95 environment have been rewritten to operate in the Windows NT environment).

Don't try to run the Windows 95 version on a PC running Windows NT. The security features built in to Windows NT does not permit the close access to your hardware that the Windows 95 version needs to properly perform diagnostic monitoring.

Although earlier versions of Norton Utilities were mainly designed for file and disk repair and recovery (what you might call fixing the problem after it breaks), the current versions are designed for monitoring your system and warning you before something breaks. The Windows 95 version enables you to perform extensive monitoring of your system's memory, disks, and files (see Figure 23.1).

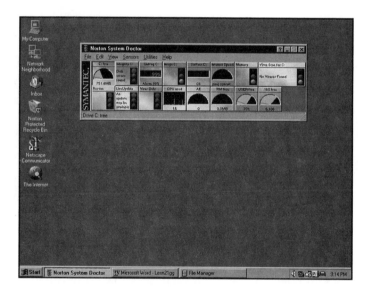

FIGURE 23.1   The Windows 95 version of Norton Utilities and some of its monitoring utilities at work.

Nuts & Bolts

A relative newcomer to the system diagnostic and recovery arena is Nuts & Bolts by Helix Software, Inc. Nuts & Bolts positions and markets itself as a Norton competitor and tries to outperform Norton in the areas of file and disk repair and system tune-up. Nuts & Bolts seems to focus more on repair than prevention and does an admirable job in disk defragmentation and file repair and recovery (see Figure 23.2). Beginning users may favor Nuts & Bolts over Norton Utilities because they may find it easier to use. It is also less expensive than Norton Utilities.

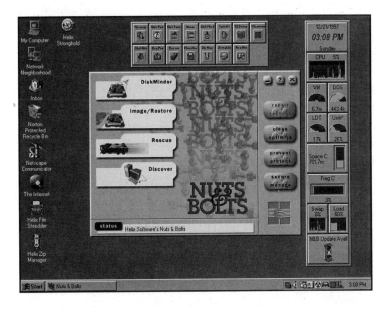

Figure 23.2 The Nuts & Bolts main interface.

Ziff-Davis WinBench97 and WinStone97

The WinBench and WinStone programs are the testing suites used by Ziff-Davis labs for all the product comparison testing that they perform for the reviews they publish. WinBench and WinStone have no diagnostic functions but are two of the best performance testing programs you can acquire.

In earlier incarnations, Ziff-Davis used to make these two utility suites available for download. Now however, the total size of the two performance testing suites has evolved to well over 130MB, and Ziff-Davis only distributes the two on CD. The good news, though, is that the cost for the CD plus shipping and handling is only $6.00. To order a copy of the latest version of WinBench and WinStone go to **http://www1.zdnet.com/zdbop/**.

WINSTONE97

WinStone97 is a comprehensive performance-testing program. It is used to test the various components in your PC against a set of relative criteria devised by Ziff-Davis labs. The tests are fairly extensive, and some may be meaningless to some beginning users. Nevertheless, WinStone97 is an excellent tool for comparing the performance of one computer against another.

WINBENCH97

WinBench97 is the companion product to WinStone97 and is used to test the performance of your PC when running a set routine of business applications. WinBench97 may be the better of the two testing suites because it tests the performance of your PC using real world applications and you get to see how your system performs while performing tasks like displaying business graphics, calculating a spreadsheet, and running a database (see Figure 23.4).

WinBench97 is most useful in enabling you to test your PC's performance before and after you upgrade components that most directly affect performance—for example, the processor and memory. Performance is rated in WinBench97 by comparing one set of results against the results generated by another computer or a computer that has been upgraded.

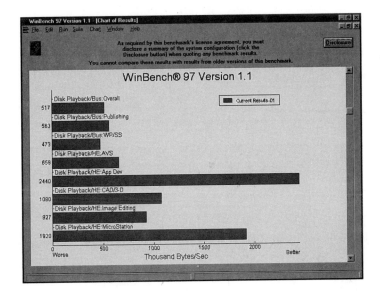

FIGURE 23.3   WinBench97 test results.

WINTUNE98

WinTune is another popular Windows performance testing program and *Windows Magazine* has recently released its 1998 version, WinTune98. WinTune98 is somewhat unique among testing programs because there is a version that you can download and run on your PC, or you can log in to the Internet, start your web browser, and run WinTune98 over the Internet from *Windows Magazine's* web site at **http://www.winmag.com/wintune98/SysTest.htm**.

WinTune98 requires a web browser capable of running ActiveX controls, which means you must use Microsoft's Internet Explorer (version 3.0 or later) to run the program. WinTune98 does not run with Netscape and the ActiveX plug-in available for download on the web.

Deactivate ActiveX controls ActiveX controls are a potential security risk, and for this reason many users deactivate ActiveX controls when using Internet Explorer. If you have ActiveX controls deactivated, you must reactivate them in order to run WinTune98.

WinTune98 performs a general systems analysis, a CPU performance test, a video system performance test, a memory test, a disk performance test, and finally, sums up everything in a report (see Figure 23.4).

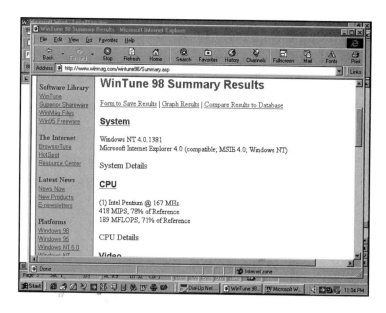

FIGURE 23.4   The WinTune98 testing summary, which is returned to you via your web browser.

OTHER TESTING UTILITIES

Other places on the web you can find similar utilities include

- *Tucows.* **http://www.tucows.com**
- *C-Net's Download and Shareware sites.* **http://www.download.com; http://www.shareware.com**
- *FileZ.* **http://www.filez.com/**
- *ZD Net Software Library.* **http://www.hotfiles.com/**
- *Windows Magazine Software Library.* **http://www.winmag.com/**
- *PC World Magazine Software Library.* **http://www.pcworld.com/software_lib/index.html**

 Bonus stuff   In addition to monitoring and diagnostic utilities, these web sites contain a wealth of programs including desktop aids, screen savers, and Internet tools.

If you don't have access to the Internet, consult your local computer salesperson for information about where you can obtain copies of these diagnostic utilities.

In this lesson, you learned about some of the software programs available to you for monitoring your PC's performance and for diagnosing problems with your PC. In the next lesson, you learn how to purchase upgrade components over the Internet.

How to Purchase Upgrade Components on the Internet

In this lesson, you learn about purchasing upgrade components for your PC over the Internet.

Purchasing on the Internet

All the PC components mentioned earlier in this book can be purchased directly over the Internet and delivered right to your front door. Although many computer users are starting to purchase items by mail order, most of the companies selling mail order are also selling over the Internet. As expected, you have to make tradeoffs when purchasing on the Internet. Some of the advantages of purchasing on the Internet are

- No sales reps are there to bother you by trying to sell you additional items that you don't want or need.

- Most companies place their entire inventory on their web site but only a fraction of it in magazines.

- You have instant access to current pricing and inventory status.

- It's very easy to do comparison shopping online.

The disadvantages to purchasing on the Internet are

- You must know what you want to purchase.
- You must purchase using a credit card.
- Many users still have concerns over Internet security.

LOCATING COMPANIES

Locating computer companies and computer supply companies who do business on the Internet is relatively easy. Look in any computer magazine and you see ads for dozens of companies and most include a web address to their online storefront. You can also locate computer companies on the Internet by using the Internet. You can use any number of search engines to locate online merchants. One of the easiest and most comprehensive listings is under Lycos. Go to the Lycos home page at **http://www.lycos .com** and follow the links: Lycos Shopping, Department Stores, Store Search, Quicksearch, Computers (see Figure 24.1).

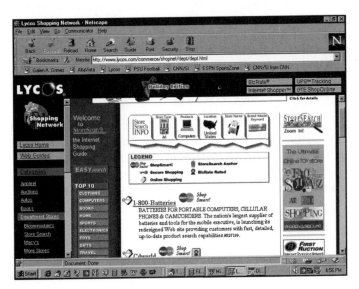

FIGURE 24.1   Computer Shopping listing under Lycos Shopping.

After you locate a few companies with whom you think you might want to do business and before you place your first order, you need to look at a few things:

- How does the company ship the order, and what do they charge? Some companies advertise what appear to be lower than competitive prices but charge you for exorbitant shipping costs to make their profit. Find out what carrier the company ships with and whether they ship overnight delivery, second-day delivery, or three- to five-day ground delivery.

- What are the company's return policies? If you order the wrong part or if the item you order does not work with your computer, can you return it? Some companies charge a five to fifteen percent restocking fee for returned items.

For online purchases, does the company use a secure web site? A secure web site is a means of conducting your transaction so that no one can tap into the communication session and see information you want to keep private, such as your credit card number. If the company is not using a secure site, make your transaction over the phone using the company's 800 number.

INTERNET SECURITY

The question of Internet security is probably the single most important factor still limiting online commerce. The main problem though is not that that the Internet commercial transactions are not secure. The main problem is that the Internet commercial transactions are not *perceived* as being secure.

What about credit card security?   If you're worried about making purchases over the Internet and giving out your credit card information online, ask yourself whether you also worry every time you eat at a restaurant and watch your waiter disappear into a back room with your credit card? You are probably safer giving your credit card number out over a secure Internet connection than you are giving your credit card to a waiter whom you've never met.

You can very easily identify whether you have a secure connection by two visible signs in your web browser. The first sign is the address of the web page you are viewing. A normal, or unsecured web page address begins **http://**, but a secure web page address begins **https://**.

The second sign that you have a secure Internet connection is some symbol or indicator from your web browser that the web site is secure. In Netscape, you see a closed lock on the toolbar across the top of the screen. In Internet Explorer, a secure web site is illustrated by a lock displayed on the status bar at the bottom of the screen.

TIPS ON BUYING PC COMPONENTS

Finally, the following tips help when you buy computer components, whether you purchase them over the Internet, call an 800 number, or simply walk into a computer store:

- Do your research first. Before you buy any item for your PC read a few product reviews comparing the item from several manufacturers. For example, if you are thinking about upgrading your CD-ROM drive, look through some recent issues of some of the major computer industry journals to see what features are considered important and what type of comparison testing has been done.

- Get recent information. Product reviews are an excellent means of getting information on products that you want to purchase, but not if the information is two years old. Computer products change rapidly. Don't bother with reviews that are more than six to eight months old. If you can't find a recent review, wait a few weeks; there will be another one.

- Make friends with the computer guru in your department or company. There is usually one person in every company who seems to know just about everything there is to know about computers. Seek out this person and become friends. Often, much of the information you need is available for the asking.

- Check UseNet (Internet Newsgroups) for comments from other users. UseNet (newsgroups) has a category for just about everything, including computer hardware. Check out comments from other users on specific brands and models. Look for comments on customer relations with a company (both the manufacturer and the dealer), to find whether the product performed as advertised and any information on problems with the product.

- Review information on upgrading in computer books such as this and others offered by Macmillan Computer Publishing.

Congratulations! You have made it through the last lesson in this book. You should now feel pretty comfortable about upgrading, purchasing, and installing the upgrade components for your PC. But don't put *Teach Yourself PC Upgrades in 10 Minutes* away on your shelf just yet. Keep it handy as a quick reference whenever you have questions about a particular PC component or upgrade question.

INDEX